D1483164

Faith, Reason, and Civilization

AN ESSAY

IN HISTORICAL ANALYSIS

BY THE SAME AUTHOR

Reflections on the Revolution of Our Time
Where Do We Go from Here?
The American Presidency
The Danger of Being a Gentleman and Other Essays
Parliamentary Government in England
The State in Theory and Practice
A Grammar of Politics
The Foundations of Sovereignty and Other Essays
Studies in Law and Politics
An Introduction to Politics
Democracy in Crisis
The Rise of European Liberalism
Karl Marx
The Socialist Tradition in the French Revolution
Authority in the Modern State
The Problem of Sovereignty
Political Thought in England from Locke to Bentham
Communism
The Dangers of Obedience and Other Essays

Faith, Reason, and Civilization

An essay in historical analysis

by

Harold J. Laski

◇◇

New York : The Viking Press

1944

THIS EDITION IS PRODUCED IN FULL COMPLIANCE WITH
ALL WAR PRODUCTION BOARD CONSERVATION ORDERS

PUBLISHED BY THE VIKING PRESS IN JUNE 1944

PUBLISHED ON THE SAME DAY IN THE DOMINION OF CANADA
BY THE MACMILLAN COMPANY OF CANADA LIMITED

PRINTED IN U.S.A. BY THE VAIL-BALLOU PRESS

To J. G. W.

with warm affection

Preface

This book, as its sub-title emphasizes, is essentially an essay and no more. To do anything like justice to the immense theme with which it deals would have taken far more time than a busy teacher can spare when, over and above his academic work, he accepts, and tries to fulfil, the duties laid upon him in this war by the fact that he is a citizen. I venture to publish it, partly because it emphasizes an aspect of the present conflict which seems to me to deserve more attention than it is receiving, and partly because it appears worth while to try and exhibit in a general way the Marxist approach to the issues with which it deals.

It owes its origin to a talk with Mr. and Mrs. Sidney Webb at Liphook, in the summer of 1939, which was itself no more than one more stage in a conversation which has lasted half my lifetime. Like so many of my generation and way of thought I owe them both a debt beyond repayment. I wish I could have had the joy of discussing it with her; a world in which she is no longer there to argue and criticize and attack one's ideas seems a much poorer world.

It owes much, too, to those long talks with my colleagues of the London School of Economics and Political Science, both teachers and pupils, who have helped to make the years of our exile from Houghton Street less hard than they would otherwise have been; among them, I must mention especially my friend H. L. Beales, whose friendship has been an endless inspiration in these grave times. I ought to say how much I have been helped in seeking to grasp the nature and problems of early Christianity by the books of my old Harvard colleague, Professor Kirsopp Lake, and, in understanding the contribution of the ancient world I was set on new lines of thought by that remarkable scholar Mr. J. M. Robertson. His *History of Free Thought* (revised ed., 2 vols., 1936) is not only a monument of learning but full of suggestion. It is to him that I owe the full realization of what was implied in the idea of the ancient world of religion as a restraint on the multitude which then takes prisoner the men who had hoped that this restraint did not bind them. And it was in talk with Robertson that I learned how this attitude to religion turned men's minds from the dream of conquering nature to the way in which in social organization the many can keep their hold over the few. It was the resemblance between the Ionian attitude to science and that of the Soviet Union which first suggested to me that the latter had found a new way of life, faith in which might well play the part supernatural creeds had played elsewhere; and it was the realization that Plato deserved the vigorous condemnation of Bacon which made me guard against the price of succumbing to the dangerous attraction of his infinite charm. Perhaps I may add—for this is at least a matter of historical interest—that when I once drew the attention of Mr. Justice Holmes to the passages in Bacon, he told me that when he was an undergraduate in Harvard College, Emerson had found him in his rooms reading the *Republic* and had drawn the reader's attention with great vigour to the criticisms in Bacon.

H. J. L.

November 1, 1943
Little Bardfield,
Essex

Contents

Faith, Reason, and Civilization

I

The Destiny of Youth

ALL over the world, the youth of this generation stand at the gates of death. In their millions, they offer a life that has hardly yet attained maturity in the service of freedom. Millions have already died for that dream; and, when the war is over, there will be millions more who, blind or deaf or maimed, will spend the remainder of their years cut off from the supreme beauties life can offer. In all the five continents, there is hardly a nation whose citizens are not suffering prison and torture, pain and hunger and toil in passionate defence of this same freedom. It is the second time within the lives of many of us that the youth of the world are asked to risk all that they have and are. They fight and toil in a conflict they did not make; the shape of its outcome is only too likely to take a form they will have little or no part in deciding. They are the victims of a fate they did not organize; and they will be sacrificed at the altar of a destiny they cannot choose.

No one who watches their achievement in the countless epics of daily battle, whether in open combat or in that more secret but not less deadly conflict of the occupied nations against their Axis taskmasters, can help feeling a sense of profound humility before the youth of our time. They go to their rendezvous with fate in a temper in which pride and courage seem equally combined. When they fail to return, their legacy is invariably a demand that those whom they leave behind shall fulfil the task they have begun. Dunkirk, Stalingrad, El Alamein, the Bataan Peninsula, the struggles, against impossible odds, in Norway and Holland and Belgium, in Greece and Yugoslavia, the seven years' war that a quarter-armed China has waged with such unbreakable resolution against Japanese aggression, all these are part of the imperishable tradition of man's effort at emancipation both from the tyranny of nature and the tyranny of authority.

Nor, in an ultimate sense, is this drama of battle superior in its revelation of the quality of man's will to be free to the passionate determination of civilian effort, wherever this has been put to the test. Nowhere have the ordinary people of the world accepted the right of the Nazi or Fascist ruler to impose himself. Everywhere, with what means they have had, they have waged, men and women alike, an unceasing war against their would-be masters which is testimony as remarkable as any in history to the supreme dignity of the human spirit. Bombardment from the air alone has cost the British people some eighty thousand lives; it has left them utterly undismayed. Hitler may have enslaved the bodies of Czechs and Poles; he has failed to establish any semblance of authority over their minds. Even where, as in Greece and Yugoslavia, the Axis powers have defeated dictators of their own pattern, they have awakened in the conquered nations a will to the revival of democracy. There has been, too, revealed in the vast struggle of the Soviet Union a power both of endurance and of organization which has given its peoples a new status in the regard of mankind. America was slow to recognize that the road to a secure freedom lay through battle; but once it entered the conflict, it mobilized its resources, both human and material, on a scale which the world has never previously seen.

The years since 1939 have been terrible years, full of evil and tragedy and waste. Yet they have also been memorable years, for they prove the capacity of men and women to serve a great cause greatly. If that capacity is wisely used it has the power to transform a bitter experience into a glorious tradition. The Axis powers are already on the way to defeat both decisive and overwhelming. But there remains for us the greater issue of seeing to it that in their defeat there is involved also the destruction of the counter-revolution for which they stand. Our victory will be thrown away unless we devote it to great ends.

II

Danger and Achievement

ANYONE who analyses the habits that have been revealed in this conflict is bound, I think, to come to certain conclusions of the first importance for our future. They are conclusions about human relationships and the implications these reveal for social theory. The war has shown us, in all its naked cruelty, the ugliness of the feelings and ideas which are demanded by the politics of power. But it has shown us also the high level men can reach when they unite together in the service of a common effort. It is not, I think, an exaggeration to say that we have discovered on a plane more adequate than ever before that mutual aid is in very truth the primary condition of self-preservation. Each of us is the stronger the deeper the solidarity of the society to which we belong; and when that solidarity is weakened, our chance of survival is weakened, too. If the common danger has proved nothing else, it has proved at least that fraternity within a commonwealth confers upon each of us a power beyond the power we possess when it is absent. No doubt it is true that in a society like our own there is no prospect of a real equality of sacrifice. But even in our gravely unequal society, the enemy of that morale which is the secret of its power to endure is the selfish man who does not see that his freedom is measured by the degree to which he shares its potentialities with others. The acquisitive citizen is a public danger in a state of siege. The man who gives the most he can to the common cause does most to create the conditions which assure his own safety.

We have learned in the hour of danger how truly we are members one of another. We have discovered that it is in the degree that we respect the claims of others, and contribute to the fulfilment of those claims, that we become capable of self-respect.

There is something almost paradoxical in a society in which an epoch of destruction, like our own, elicits from literally millions of citizens not only an effort to serve their fellows, but the discovery that there is latent in most of them a joy in service which satisfies their impulses in a degree far higher, for most, than the performance of their normal routine of life. I have known, for example, a journalist who, as a sailor on a minesweeper, found in the dramatic danger of his work an exhilaration he had never found in the daily routine of his newspaper; and he was, before the war, a journalist of real distinction. I have met wardens in the A.R.P. service to whom the forgetfulness of self that came in a period of danger offered fulfilment that they had never known in their business life. And as a university teacher I have found, in these years of war, a passionate desire among students to understand the social problems which confronted them which made not only the quality of their own effort, but, not less, the excitement of teaching, something far beyond what I have experienced in those days of peace when the chief concern of each student was less the meanings of the problems he was discussing than the career to which he might look in terms of the class he obtained in his degree. I do not think it is untrue to say that there are few people, in proportion to the whole citizen-body, who have not sought in these years of danger the chance to do some service beyond the effort they deemed a reasonable one in the years of peace.

That little of all this has been an unmixed altruism I do not for a moment deny. It is obvious that there have entered into the effort it all represents motives of the most varied kinds. Vanity, the desire for power, a sense of shame in being useless—no doubt all of these are a living part of the anxiety to do something that is more than safeguarding one's own interest. Man is not less capable of enjoying self-display and power in a critical time than he is when danger is absent; indeed, it may well be true that the drama of great events is more capable of evoking those qualities than a period when emergence from the routine of privacy is more likely to produce surprise than gratitude from one's fellow-citizens. Certainly a successful politician or a successful soldier is more likely to secure the sense of fulfilment when what he does arrests a universal attention than in an age when his effort will remain in large degree unnoticed by those on whose behalf he labours; perhaps there is no glory more satisfying to those who love the applause of the crowd. But when all allowance has been made for the satisfaction of this love of fame or power, it still remains true that in this conflict quite literally there are men and women by the hundred thousand who have done brave deeds not for the glory they would win but because their self-respect would not have permitted them to act otherwise. We are faced by the seeming paradox that war, which unleashes all that is most brutal in human nature, unleashes in it also the utmost limits of heroism of which men are capable. So that while it is dull and ugly and cruel, the expression for most who experience it of a monstrous routine in which they are mostly conscious of a sort of mechanical degradation, it also brings to some of those engaged in it, civilians now, as well as fighting men, a sense of fulfilment far more profound than anything they are likely to experience in the normal round of their daily lives. And for those to whom that sense of fulfilment comes there remains a memory which survives all the pain and loss they have endured; just as there are moments in love which, in memory, outweigh by their splendour a score of years of suffering.

War compels the organization of mutual aid as the inescapable price of victory. A people cannot win that is not at one with itself, which does not hold the great ends of life in common. That has been illustrated supremely by the experience of France in this war. Hitler did not defeat it in the six tragic weeks from May 10, 1940; it was beaten in the long years between the first World War and the outbreak of the second when men like Pétain and Laval grew into preference for a victory of property over freedom. A great army, no doubt, like that of Hitler must be met by an opponent which fights it on equal terms in vital matters of material equipment. But it cannot be fought on equal terms by an opponent who is either uncertain that he wants to win or unable to look with confidence to the morrow of victory. Once it is apparent that a government is unwilling to pay the price that victory demands, it invites defeat more certainly than through any other cause. But a government can only pay that price when it is confident of national unity behind it. Without that unity, it can only be saved either by the chance possession of a great military genius or by overwhelming material superiority. If either is lacking, like Russia in 1917 or France in 1940, it is, in fact, beaten before it enters the battle. The defeat may be delayed; its advent may even escape the notice of those whose business it is to watch for the approach of danger, as Lord Milner missed the signs of revolution in Russia, and as General Gamelin failed to see that the power of which he disposed was broken before he sought to use it.

And national unity, in the modern world, is built upon the will to make an idea victorious. Dynastic wars are outmoded; even wars the makers of which are searching for personal fame have ceased to have a meaning in our time. The wars we wage are an effort to break an idea the enemy seeks to impose upon us; and we can only break his idea by our own possession of an idea he is himself unable to destroy. That is the significance, to take an obvious example, of the contrast between the idea Mr. Chamberlain symbolized and the idea embodied in Mr. Winston Churchill. So long as Mr. Chamberlain was Prime Minister the unity of the nation was disproportionate to the problems it confronted, not because Mr. Chamberlain or the nation did not want to win, but because neither he nor the nation, when he led it, had any real grasp of the power he was fighting, or of the need to build the call to action upon a foundation as challenging as the Hitler idea itself. Mr. Chamberlain had a general support from the masses; but there was lacking in that support the inner and intimate conviction that he was fighting their war. No one, I think, can doubt that, while he was in Downing Street, there was an absence in the scale and intensity of the effort over which he presided, of the passion that a great idea communicates. The will to win, no doubt, was there; but it was not a will informed by the kind of intense determination which was infused into it the moment Mr. Churchill became Prime Minister.

We may differ about the reasons for its absence. Something of it, no doubt, was due to the contrast between the personalities of the two men. To Mr. Chamberlain the need to embark upon conflict was the public announcement that his policy was a failure; to Mr. Churchill, it was the fulfilment of a passionate prophecy which had, by its informing idea, excluded him for long years from public life as a Minister of the Crown. The nation, I think, felt that, however pure the motives of Mr. Chamberlain, he could not put the whole of his heart into the task of organizing victory; there was always, somewhere, at the back of his mind, the sense of a vague hope that he could come to an accommodation with the enemy. But, when Mr. Churchill took his place, not even the days of supreme danger left the masses in doubt that the hour had found the man. The astonishing phenomenon in the first six months of Mr. Churchill's premiership is that though it was accompanied by disasters as great as any since the grim days of Austerlitz and Jena, the danger brought exhilaration rather than fear, hope rather than frustration. That was in part because Mr. Churchill represented to the masses, even though it took him long to symbolize it for his own party, the idea that, cost what it might, the overthrow of Hitlerism was the supreme object of policy. And closely connected with that view was the popular recognition, superbly embodied in Mr. Churchill's speeches, that whatever changes in the national life were necessary for victory, their necessity would be accepted by his Government.

It is, in short, no matter of pride, but a simple statement of the facts, that, with the assumption of the premiership by Mr. Churchill, there was something akin to a spiritual renaissance in Britain. All the world waited breathlessly for its invasion and its overthrow; no foreign power, least of all Germany and Italy, doubted that it was merely postponing surrender for a few weeks for the sake of its prestige. But as the summer passed into the autumn, and, in its turn, the autumn passed into the long winter nights in which, from dusk to day, the people endured a pitiless bombardment from the air, it began to dawn upon the world that there was a reserve of strength in the British people which no disaster seemed able to exhaust. The very depth, indeed, of the danger seemed to evoke from ordinary men and women a resilience that neither fatigue nor defeat could overcome. They gave their energy and devotion in a measure which it would be insolent to praise. And there was revealed a reserve of capacity in organization, as in the air raids, and a fund of heroism which it had been difficult to suspect existed in the years of semi-panic before 1940. Mr. Churchill had asked, at the supreme moment of crisis, that the people of Britain should so comport themselves that the future historian would acclaim this period as its finest hour. In the great year from the fall of France to the entrance of Russia into the war not even he could have expected a fuller measure of response.

I do not claim for the British people any quality of devotion more profound than was displayed by the Soviet Union after 1941, or by the armed forces of the United States when, in the winter of that year, Japanese aggression and treachery brought them also into the war. What it is essential for my purpose to emphasize is that men and women the normal routine of whose lives seemed to lack any character of heroic proportions became, as it were overnight, capable of exertions and of sacrifice which little in the inter-war years would have led one to predict. Even when one makes allowance for that proportion of each people which was selfish and lazy, and sought, so far as it could, to evade the obligations for which the period called, the remarkable number of those who sought the chance of service, the degree in which habits were adapted to an experience entirely novel in its intensity, these remain impressive. Above all, I think, what is outstanding in these years is the discovery by men and women whose status in life was comfortable that there was something wrong in the foundations of a civilization in which the things they took for granted were, for the great mass of the nation, unheard-of luxuries of which they never ceased to talk. No doubt there were, in the evacuation, for example, irritations and evasions and annoyances about which there exists a whole literature, in sociology as well as fiction. But alongside these there must be put the millions who learned, for the first time, the beauties of the sea and of the countryside, the effort to make the life of the rural areas a thing that the dweller in a city slum did not at once desert, the real imaginative insight represented by the new factories, the achievement of rationing which made the standard of health and diet in wartime as good in Britain as in the days of peace.

I speak of Britain only because, naturally enough, I know the conditions in Britain best. But it is clear from reliable observers that the achievement of the Soviet Union yields nothing to that of Britain. It is clear that there have been episodes of heroism in Greece and Yugoslavia, in Holland and Norway, in Belgium and in Poland, which will last as long as the memory of man. Lidice has become a part of the folk-lore of the world; and those half-armed Jews who, in the ghetto of Warsaw, made their Nazi taskmasters, with tanks and aeroplanes and heavy guns, give life for life before they died, make one realize that the tradition of Judas Maccabeus still proudly lives. Nor may an Englishman omit to note the courage with which in every occupied country men of the United Nations have been passed, at the risk of life, from house to house until they reached some frontier of safety. And I imagine that even the most truculent Conservative can hardly read unmoved the story of the execution of the brave French Communist, Gabriel Péri, as a hostage in Paris. Every one of the peoples who fight Hitlerism in this war builds from its agony a tradition in which the elements of immortality are unmistakable.

III

The Paradox of Victory

When one contrasts the years of cynicism and disillusion between the wars with the character of the war years themselves, not even the horror that the war years have brought can prevent the former from seeming, somehow, pitiful by comparison. For these since 1939 have been a fight for freedom, and the conflict has had about it a directness and simplicity absent from the years of peace. For it is, after all, intelligible enough that nations, if they can, should fight with passion against the razing of their cities to the dust, and the forcible captivation of their citizens into workers for the enemy who has destroyed them. What is most difficult in this sense, during the war, that we march down a road at the end of which is liberation, is the uncertainty whether, when we have reached its end, it is indeed freedom that we shall attain. For when we meet the enemy freedom creates a terrible paradox it is not easy to resolve. There is undoubtedly a sense of profound emancipation for us all in the very fact of his defeat; to rekindle the lights of Europe will seem like a new dawn. But his defeat is rather the condition upon which freedom can be won than freedom itself in the sense of a power in the ordinary citizen of self-affirmation.

For we have, if we are honest, to admit that to return to 1939 is not to confer this power of self-affirmation upon any but a tiny minority in each of the United Nations. We realize without difficulty the barbarism implicit in a statement like that of Dr. Ley, the chief of the German Labour Front: "A lower race," he wrote, "needs less room, less clothing, less food, and less culture than a higher race. The German cannot live in the same fashion as the Pole and the Jew. . . . More bread, more clothes, more living room, more culture, more beauty, these our race must have or it dies."[1] If Poland, for instance, went back merely to its pre-war condition, the level of both its hygiene and nutrition would be so low as to assure the recurrence of typhus, a disease which is always associated with dirt and poverty.[2] Sir John Orr has calculated that we need to double the food production of the world to attain an adequate level of food consumption. The expectation of life of an Indian ryot is today barely half that of an Englishman. And even in the United States, the richest country in the world, and the one whose productive capacity is least likely to be impaired by the war, investigation has shown that, in the field of agriculture alone, there is a population of some four million migratory labourers and their families who lack sufficient food and clothing, who are barely literate, and live in housing conditions as bad as the worst of European slums.[3] The freedom to which they return with the defeat of Hitlerism is less broad and convincing than the rhetoric of our statesmen is inclined to admit.

A war of this magnitude brings us up against the ultimate things. Few people believe any longer that a liberal economic system is likely to achieve prosperity for the masses. On the contrary, the inter-war years have shown few things more clearly than that it breeds an excessive prosperity in the few and an excessive poverty in the many. And that contrast tends to beget, as Disraeli said, two nations within a single society, which rarely speak the same language and rarely know how to maintain a unity of outlook. Indeed, the contrast, as very notably in the first third of this century in the United States, tends to create a comparison so startling that the main preoccupation of the rich man, is, in part, how to invest what he does not know how to spend, and, in part, to make the state-power an instrument to protect his wealth. The result is the simple and inevitable one that the possessions of the rich breed in them that temper of power which is poisonous to themselves and to the poor of whose

---

1 Quoted in G. H. Bourne, *Starvation in Europe* (London, 1943), p. 17.

2 *Ibid.*, p. 23.

3 H. Collins, *America's Own Refugees* (Princeton, 1942).

envy they live in constant fear. It makes the society not a fellowship of equals, but a collection of masters and slaves; and its ambitions are those set not by the quest for that perfection which is the sole way to elevate a society, but by the imitation of what the most successful men among its members desire. So Sir Ernest Cassel, we are told, must buy expensive pictures and objects of art though he had no interest in them save as they proved his power to outbid a rival in a field where fashion demanded his interest; and Mr. Henry C. Folger amassed first folios of Shakespeare to demonstrate his pre-eminence in an area where only the wealthy can obtain admission. We have only to compare, say, the conception of freedom in the Funeral Oration of Pericles or the Gettysburg speech of Lincoln with the habits of the wealthy class in our plutocracy to see that the pursuit of perfection is omitted from their concept of life.

A war, this is to say, which had no other result than the defeat of the aggressors might create the conditions in which freedom and democracy were possible, but it would not be an assurance that either would be realized. For it is, broadly speaking, true of the plutocracy in each of the United Nations that, as Bagehot wrote of the French *noblesse* of the eighteenth century, their lives "describe a life unsuitable to such a being as man in such a world as the present one; in which there are no high aims, no severe duties, where some precept of morals seems not so much to be sometimes broken, as to be generally suspended, and forgotten—such a life, in short, as God has never suffered men to lead on the earth long, which He has always crushed out by calamity or revolution." And if it be said that Bagehot was writing in an ugly period in which the fierceness of the competitive system forbade the search for grace and beauty, the answer, I think, is the final one that the two generations which succeeded the age in which Bagehot wrote had, for the most part, the inheritance of security without the effort involved in attaining it. A world which turned from the performance of a genuine public service to the fierce pursuit of some exotic sensation had lost the high ardour which gives its authority a natural character. It turns art into the Royal Academy; it makes the opera a social function rather than a musical performance. It offers a lofty patronage to poets or priests who are willing to forget the high end they have to serve if only they can be invited to the right houses. "Sidney Smith talking," Carlyle wrote in his diary, "other persons prating, jargoning; to me, through these thin cobwebs, Death and Eternity sat glaring."

What Carlyle wrote with his typical fury over a century ago, almost any critic could have written in the inter-war years. Nor was it an answer to his indignation that, in the interval, it had become the mode to lend to charity the perfume of the aristocratic presence. For it was the assumption which lay behind that charity that it justified the acceptance of what William James so rightly called the "bitch goddess success." In the 'seventies to the 'nineties of the last century men read how Mr. Rockefeller bought judges and corrupted legislatures with a passionate sense of indignation; twenty years later the propaganda skill of Mr. Ivy Lee had made his superfluous millions into a symbol through which Mr. Rockefeller was numbered among the benefactors of the human race. The Carnegie of the Homestead strike was a reckless adventurer who climbed to security over the low wages and long hours of thousands of helpless immigrants. But the Carnegie who scattered public libraries over half of Britain and offered the poor boy in Scotland that chance in a university which the state should have organized had become an eminent philanthropist upon whose benevolence politicians like John Morley and John Burns were proud to depend in their declining years. As one looks back upon it all, one has no difficulty in accepting the defiant judgment of William Morris: "A civilisation which I *know* now is destined to perish: what a joy to think of."

There is a sense in which Morris' insight into the future was prophetic; the civilization which aroused in him the fury of a man to whom its incompatibility with beauty was obvious was, within twenty years of his death, to rush headlong into war. Thereby it made it clear that the nations of the world had marched into a cul-de-sac from which there was no exit but by force. Yet, in that first World War, the two outstanding things are, first, the incredible heroism of ordinary people, their endurance, their power to sacrifice themselves, their limitless devotion to a cause in which they believe, and, second, the inability of the statesmen in the victorious nations to use their triumph for a great end. No one can analyse the years of conflict from 1914 to 1918 without a deep sense of the contrast between the level of individual morality and that of the state's behaviour. Not even the thirty million or so of casualties which the war of 1914 cost persuaded the men who held power at, and after, Versailles to recognize the claims of reason to its empire over the minds of men. America entered upon that ugly epoch in which, under Harding and Coolidge and Hoover, the White House became a kind of annex of Wall Street. Britain moved, after the first feverish passion of a khaki election, into an era in which no Conservative Government could ever offer sufficient concessions to possess effective authority, and no Labour Government ever had the courage to act upon the principles it professed. A frustrated Italy exchanged the democratic institutions it had scarcely known for a dictator whose power was built upon the acquiescence of the privileged classes in his gangsterism. France saw its triumph fade into a disillusion in which it was uncertain whether to be more afraid of the threat from without or the threat from within. The early promise of a German renaissance was soon dissipated by the realization that, behind the façade of the Weimar Republic, the same forces whose ambitions had been the occasion of the first World War were moving into power through forms even more ugly than the empire of William II had known. And Japan, with a remorseless energy of which the depth was revealed by the fact that not even the inscrutable East can hide mass assassination, was seeking to build the foundations of an empire which should be to the East what Rome had been to the Ancient World. Of the major powers which battled against one another in the war of 1914 only Russia can be truly said to have learned the meaning of its implications; and it was not until the world discovered, to its own amazement, what Russia had become in the second World War that the significance of its revolution became generally understood by the statesmen of our time.

Anyone who reads in our time the rescript of Valentinian III which permitted practice to the African lawyers driven from their homes by the Vandal invasion will be tempted to think that there lies behind it a tragedy not dissimilar from the contemporary problem of the refugees. Invasion brought with it the catastrophes invariably involved in its disorder, sudden poverty and widespread disrespect for law, and the revelation that there is deep-seated corruption in the administration of the Empire. But as one examines more carefully the causes which led to the downfall of the imperial system, it becomes ever more obvious that the success of the Barbarian invasion was less a cause than an effect of the fall of the Western Empire. It is evident that the civil service of the provinces was little less than a body of brigands. The wealthy were not only increasing their possessions, but they were evading the taxes it was their obligation to pay. The senatorial class, like the nobility of the *ancien régime* in France, had, for the most part, status and property without corresponding functions. After the age of Diocletian, the decay in the quality of local government is one of the outstanding features of the Empire; and the position of a person of curial descent was not easy to distinguish from that of hereditary servitude. The cruel burden which fell upon the small proprietor was only equalled by the harshness of provincial governors and the corruption of the tax-collector. The courts of justice deliberately favoured the wealthy. The lot of the serf was so hard that it was clearly not unusual for him to fly from the estate to which he belonged. The Roman world seemed to Saint Jerome to be sinking into ruin; and it is a Christian writer, Salvianus, who bemoans the inability of his faith to regenerate the Empire. The wealthy, for him, are as limitless in their passion for riches and luxury as they are brutal in their oppression of the poor. Political convulsion seems to combine with intellectual decay to wreck the foundations of the Roman civilization.[1]

No one can reflect upon the age which saw the final eclipse of Rome, can catch, for instance, the note almost of imminent doom in the great epic of Claudian, without the sense of immersion in an irretrievable tragedy. And yet we know that even while we seem to be watching a setting sun, there is creeping slowly towards us the light of a new day. It comes indeed with painful slowness, and the price for its arrival is a heavy one. *"Mieux vaut le soldat que le prêtre,"* wrote Renan,[2] *"car le soldat n'a aucun prétention métaphysique."* But the priest, if he brings with him the tyranny of a dogma, brings with him, also, the exhilaration of an idea. It is the achievement of the Christian Church that, with all its weaknesses, and in despite alike of its contempt for history and its willingness to compromise with the secular power, it gradually gave birth to a revival of hope among mankind. And that revival was, in its origins, the work of humble men who are regarded with contempt by the great Empire they challenged. They were not very consistent, and it was not until a relatively late period in the evolution of their doctrine that they attracted men of learning to their service. No one can read the Old Testament without the sense that it comes from a people to whom the gospel of hard work was vital; just as it is hard to read the New Testament and discover in the central figure of its narrative any deep concern with a workaday world. Compared to Plato or Aristotle, to Seneca or to Cicero, the great writers of the Bible lack the sophistication of the professional thinker. Yet, at their greatest, as with Amos or the second Isaiah, with the author of the Book of Job or with Saint Paul, they have a quality of eternal inspiration which belongs only to the supreme figures in literature. They write, no doubt, in a world of slaves; and their tradition is rooted in that Jewish culture which was not looked upon with satisfaction, perhaps even with interest, by the imperial favourites who won from

---

[1] Cf. S. Dill, *Roman Society in the Last Century of the Western Empire* (ed. Af. 1910).

[2] *Histoire du peuple d'Israël,* II, 501.

their master an appointment as governor in one of the dependencies of Rome. Yet the magic of their alchemy was such that they could not only promise regeneration to an Empire in decline; by the age of Constantine they had come to dominate the whole outlook of the Western world.

IV

Ideas as Acts

ANYONE who watches the slow, almost agonizing, triumph of Christianity over its rivals in the first three centuries of its history must often have speculated on the causes of its victory. To anyone who does not accept its miraculous elements as a matter of faith, its victory must have seemed both difficult and even bewildering. It was, in large degree, the faith of a class which was held in contempt by the men who ruled Rome. It had no interest in, was even antagonistic to, the knowledge they possessed of the cause of things. In so far as it sought to satisfy the needs and aspirations of the needy and the humble, Mithraism was a powerful rival perhaps until such a period as the beginning of the fourth century; and it is evident from the literature that the votaries of Mithras did not succumb without a struggle. And most of the literature which has survived from the epoch between the Second Punic War and the final triumph of the Christian Church is an unhappy amalgam of despair and suffering. The world is seen to be an unrighteous world, mysterious, cruel, insecure. All the foundations of the Græco-Roman civilization were felt to be cracking, and it is obvious that few periods of which we have knowledge could have been more tragic than this until the final eclipse of its principles has made its culture seem irrelevant to the imposition of a working faith upon mankind.

Then comes the Christian victory; and, despite the fall of Rome itself, it is a victory which is able, century after century, to extend the boundaries of its conquest. Slowly, but with a triumphant certainty, a new faith sweeps over Western civilization, enabling its votaries to overcome their sense of despair and to find a new confidence in the future. What are the bases of this victory? It was clear that no new faith had any chance of enduring unless it was capable of making an appeal to the masses which, ignorant and poor, felt bitterly the injustice of a world in which blind fortune seemed to reward neither effort nor virtue. It was clear, also, that the new faith must make an appeal to that *élite* which, like the philosophers and lawyers whom Stoicism so profoundly moved, felt, hardly less than the poor, that virtue established an unanswerable claim to justice. No new faith could hope for success which was national merely; the imperialism of Rome demanded a religion as universal as the dominion it had exercised. And no new faith was likely to make its way which lacked the power to absorb those older doctrines, items of belief in which were as old as the peoples of the Mediterranean; merely to be novel in the realm of faith is always to outrage rather than to persuade. The new faith, finally, must have had the power to elevate its votaries, to satisfy the moral impulse of man, above all to prevent that sense of frustration which left him with a sense that he was alone and helpless in a hostile universe he could not hope to change.

The victory of Christianity over its rivals was the outcome of its ability to meet these tests. No doubt, it had to fight its way to victory; no doubt, also, the price it paid for success was high. But the central fact in the movement to its triumph is unmistakable. It is the recovery by man of belief in himself. Whatever our view of the theology by which that recovery was achieved, however convinced we may be that its chief elements are unhistorical, the fact is that it was a recovery. And the result, in the long run, was to create an atmosphere of hope instead of despair, of effort instead of resignation. The victory of Christianity over paganism meant a revitalization of the human mind. It was not merely that it killed a mass of ugly superstitions; no doubt in doing so it begat a body of superstitions of its own. What was important was that it enabled men to face the future affirmatively instead of negatively. It gave them the conviction that, despite the burden of the struggle they must endure, in the end they were certain of salvation. It is in the contribution of that certainty, and by reason of the impulses it emphasized in man as a member of society, that Christianity was able to play its part in regenerating the fabric of the ancient civilization.

I do not think anyone can examine with care our contemporary situation without being constantly reminded that we again require some faith that will revitalize the human mind. Almost as clearly as in the declining days of the Roman Empire, our scheme of values seems to have broken down. Scientific advance, material progress, an immense widening of the horizons of knowledge, not all of these together have been able to maintain a sense of confidence about the future. On the contrary, this second World War is the climax of an era of frustration in which the conflict over the values to be maintained was as ugly and as cynical as at any period since the Reformation. The belief in progress declined from a principle of social action to the status of a private Utopianism which the historian analysed in much the same way as he studied the erosion of a belief in the doctrine of a social contract. The idea that the end of society was to fulfil the inherent dignity of human personality, an idea which, for at least a century, had sought to transcend the barriers of birth and race, of wealth and creed, began to give way before the idea that the masses are unfit for power, that there is no more than a small *élite* with the capacity required for its exercise. Both fraternity and equality were at a heavy discount everywhere; and even the idea of freedom was looked upon as a commodity which every wise government would carefully ration among its citizens. In each nation, a small class lived in a luxury as fantastic in comparison as that of the Roman aristocrat compared with the plebs in the latter days of the Empire; and if bread and circuses were the price of privilege in Rome, the social services were the ransom paid by the rich of our own time to maintain an inert apathy among the masses about those matters of social constitution it is always dangerous to encourage them to examine.

The breakdown of our scheme of values was apparent on every hand. It was seen in the grim recrudescence of power politics; only a moral bankruptcy could explain the acceptance of men like Mussolini and Hitler as the heads of great nations. It was seen in the economic world; the great depression is significant not merely because it permitted the existence of millions of unemployed at a time when our technological mastery over nature advanced by leaps and bounds. It is significant, even more, because, with its advent, America ceased to be the land of promise and revealed that its foundations were no different in final character from those of the old world. It is significant, still more, because, when the "first fine careless rapture" of the New Deal —which lasted just one hundred days—was over, the economic royalists of the United States became the passionate opponents of every principle by the fulfilment of which America had become an article in the faith of mankind. The world will not remember the achievements of the New Deal so clearly as its historian will emphasize that, to Wall Street and to State Street, President Roosevelt was the chief figure in an undeclared civil war fought by his enemies with a venomous passion the United States had not seen since the conflict between North and South.

America ceased, after the first World War, to be the land of promise. It was not less important in the field of economics and politics, that, all over the world, socialist parties became what they called "realistic," which was, in fact, a term by which they concealed their doubts of whether it was worth while to fight for their socialism. There were Labour Governments in Great Britain in 1924 and 1929; neither of them even dreamed that a socialist transformation of society was open to it. And, not less important, when the Labour Party was in opposition, its main concern was less to fight for its principles as Parnell, for example, had shown that the parliamentary system could be used to compel new orientations, than to establish a reputation for safety and soundness with the very sections of the population which had a vested interest in the defeat of socialism.

What is true of the Labour Party in Parliament is true also of the trade-union leaders from whose outlook its main ethos derived. Before 1914, their outlook was geared to that of the working class from which they came. Their habits of mind, their

ambitions, both political and economic, were set in a working-class frame; and their wives and children did not dream of a future outside the working class. After 1919, the trade-union leaders were essentially the civil service of the trade unions; their contact with their members was a contact in office hours. Their social life was on a plane largely defined by the employers with whom they negotiated. Their wives lived the typical life of the middle-class *bourgeoise* of the suburbs; and their children went from the universities into the ordinary professional careers. They even resented the growth of a socialist membership in the Labour Party which was not rooted in the trade unions they controlled; and they rarely suspected that a change in the character of capitalist organization demanded a proportionate adjustment of trade-union organization. By the outbreak of the second World War, they found it easier to maintain good relations with the civil servants of the *bourgeois* state than to adjust their outlook to that of those among their own members who thought it the central mission of the working class to advance to the possession of political power.

The history of France and Germany only differs from that of Great Britain in the fact that it was more tragic. In neither, when the supreme test came, did the workers, either through their political or their economic organizations, make even the attempt to defeat the agents of counter-revolution. In Germany, the most powerful socialist movement which, outside the Soviet Union, the world has so far seen collapsed with a completeness which was only surpassed by the humility with which the trade unions not only accepted destruction at the hands of their conqueror, but even watched him organize a war which meant their decisive annihilation with less spirit of defiance than their predecessors had shown in 1848, when their organization was in its infancy. Socialists had held office under the Weimar Republic, but they had lacked even the energy to fight the movement which consciously avowed that it sought their destruction. One has only to compare the passionate faith of the men who wrote the "Communist Manifesto" nearly a century ago with the tepid abasement of the successors who accepted the advent of Hitler to power, or, like Severing in Berlin, surrendered power to an infantry platoon, to realize the abyss between them which had been dug in the intervening years. In 1919, at least, there were Liebknecht and Rosa Luxembourg; in 1933 the German masses awaited a signal from their leaders which never came.

If the overthrow of the Third French Republic in 1940 was the result of swift defeat in battle, there are yet two comments to be made upon it. The vitality of the French people had not only been sapped by the costly holocaust of the first World War; even more, the vitality of their democratic institutions was destroyed in the interval between the two world wars by men who did not doubt that property is preferable to freedom.[1] And when the surrender came, though there were French socialist leaders, above all Léon Blum, whose defiance of the men who betrayed France was in the great tradition, there were others who did not know their executioner even when he placed the rope about their neck. No one can fail to see that the defeat of France was the outcome rather of bad leadership than of popular pusillanimity; the speed with which Frenchmen began to organize resistance after the surrender is proof of that. But in the last decade of the Republic it is impossible not to detect a loss of moral fibre, an unwillingness to face hard facts, an undercurrent of corruption and weakness which tried to make the best of both worlds. Nowhere is there that freedom from moral fear in the face of the enemy which is the condition upon which alone victory can be organized. The Commune in the aftermath of defeat in 1870, Vichy as the outcome of defeat seventy years later, that contrast, I think, measures the change in spirit in the two periods. And the France of Vichy is the logical outcome of a long evolution; it is wholly misread if we do not relate it not merely to military disaster but also to profound habits deeply rooted in the French *bourgeoisie*. It must be set in the

---

[1] Cf. D. W. Brogan, *The Development of the Third Republic* (London, 1940). This masterly analysis is the more revealing since it was completed before the fall of France.

context of February 6, 1934, of the Dreyfus case, of *Boulangisme;* and these, in their turn, are closely connected with the tawdry Second Empire, with the *coup d'état* which preceded it, with the June days of 1848. And there is an important sense in which the breakdown of the Second Republic, and the choice of Louis Napoleon as its inheritor, marks nothing so much as the protest of *bourgeois* society against the men and the ideas in whose fulfilment would have been found the completion of the great purposes of 1789. When Hitler defeated France in 1940, it was hardly less a victory for the principles of the *ancien régime* than for Germany.

V

◇◇

The Recovery of Faith

THE most important war aim that is before us is the recovery of a faith by which we can all of us stand. It needs to be more than the faith in the right of the nation to which we belong to an independent existence. Men, no doubt, have died proudly for their native land; and it would be a poor sort of civilization in the future which could not find room for the full independence of national cultures. Their very diversity, indeed, is one of the surest ways of making our civilization rich in creative vigour and eager to respond to significant individual experience. But a faith in one's nation is not enough. That is partly because scientific discovery has made the national idea in large part obsolete in matters of economic and political concern; but it is partly, also, because no faith can create in the individual the kind of values we require if he surrenders his judgment to the keeping of any organization, be it nation or Church or party. Every one of us has one obligation which goes deeper than the obligation we owe to the collective relations in which the fact of community life involves us; that obligation is to that inner self in each one of us which we can never yield to anyone's keeping without ceasing to be true to our dignity as human beings. The faith, therefore, that puts the nation first is inadequate unless it is prepared to sit in judgment upon the acts that are done in the nation's name. To rejoice in victory as such is never enough; it is imperative to be sure, as an individual citizen, that the victory is for a cause one's inner self approves. For a faith that is built upon a service that is mechanical and not dynamic, while it may contribute to the power it serves, contributes blindly and without that intimate understanding which alone enables faith to create values which can endure. The blind passion for nationalism that has been so widespread over the world since the first partition of Poland has wrought at least as much evil as good for civilization; and there is evidence and to spare that, in the special conditions of our epoch, it may easily take us down a road which leads to wholesale disaster. We can see that without difficulty where the German citizen offers unquestioning obedience to the orders of Hitler and his Nazis, or in that fantastic perversion of patriotism which makes Japanese citizens think they are serving their country when they extend the poison of the opium traffic in occupied China. But what applies to German nationalism or to Japanese applies in principle to any other brand. None of us can escape the moral responsibility of personal decision; and we must learn that the very refusal to decide which makes a blind obedience possible is not less our own decision because we have willed our conscience into the keeping of another. Evasion of choice is itself a form of choice.

There is little reason to suppose that the recovery of a system of values in our civilization would be the outcome of a revival of faith in the supernatural. For, in the first place, there is little reason to suppose that any ecclesiastical organization has now a sufficient hold to act as a means of turning men's effort from force to persuasion. There has been, indeed, historically, a deeper habit of peace in China, where supernatural religion has played but a small part, than in Europe or the rest of Asia, where its hold has been immense. And, in any case, outside the Society of Friends, and a small body of mystic cults, the two thousand years of Christian history suggest that religious creeds are subdued to nationalisms, and even to political opinions, rather than that they possess the power to transcend them. And this is a factor quite apart from the philosophic and historical objections to which all organized forms of the Christian faith give rise. Even if some Christian Church were able to secure acceptance of its principles in Europe and America, it would leave unsolved the problem of the relevance of its dogmas to the other non-Christian world religions. We should then, if we put our trust in the Christian religion as the source of a revival of values, either have to seek its imposition by force upon those who rejected its principles, or find some terms of accommodation between Christianity and its chief alternatives which would drive us, at the end, into something like the civil religion which Rousseau recommended as the unifying cement of state organization. But no one would seriously recommend a return to an age of religious persecution save a handful of fanatics who, like Franco and his like in Spain, have an ulterior end to serve which most of us would regard as wholly incompatible with the Christian spirit; while it is in a high degree unlikely that a devout believer in Christianity, or Hinduism, or Mohammedanism, would see its special character lost in a general declaration of faith which builds upon the rejection of the peculiar dogmas on which they base their creed. It has been, in any case, impossible, since the time of Bayle, seriously to accept the view that the social quality of the citizen depends upon his acceptance of religious dogmas in any sense which claims for these an ecclesiastical sanction.

VI

The Substance of Faith

If we are to build anew a scheme of values in society we must look in other directions. We must begin with the assumption that the sole method open to mankind by which he can improve his lot is an increasing mastery of nature. In the degree only of our scientific knowledge is there any hope of release from the material fetters which still weigh upon the vast majority of men. That assumption, of course, itself rests upon a faith. It believes in the power of knowledge, in the need, therefore, to maximize its communication. It is compelled, accordingly, to insist that Plato was right when he said that the true test of a state is whether it regards its minister of education as more important than its minister of war. It follows that, to meet this test, the state, so to say, must not only provide each of its citizens with a map of the universe about which he has to find his way, but must also give him the means of assuring himself that he can use the map with which he is provided. That means something more than a general system of formal education. For no serious theory of pedagogy today would separate the school from the home, or the home from the diet which makes the child capable of learning in school. But, once more, if the school and the home are twin sides of a single experience, it is obvious that the state is bound to interest itself directly and profoundly in the conditions upon which the home itself depends. From a civic angle, this means at once that economic security, decent wages, and reasonable hours of labour are all matters which, through their effect upon the parents, concern the education of the child. When all allowance is made for the high probability that the extraordinary child will triumph over all difficulties of an inadequate environment, it remains vital for us to remember that the extraordinary child is rare. Most of us are destined to be very much what our conditions make us; and not even the uniqueness of each of us justifies the state in assuming that we shall learn from life what our intelligence and character and temperament fit us to learn. That was why Renan was justified in claiming that, with all the risks and limitations involved, *"l'homme formé selon ces disciplines vaut mieux en définitive que l'homme instinctif des âges de foi."* It is true, as he said, that no one is rendered poorer if you take bad money from his purse. Ignorance forcibly preserved, knowledge to which access lies over a steep and difficult road, these are methods for the destruction of individuality. And both the Christian and the non-Christian can at least join hands in supporting what has perhaps been the main contribution of Christianity to social progress, the passionate affirmation of the right of each human being to fulfil his individuality.

It is, surely, in this affirmation only that the sources of a new faith for the post-war generation can be found. And as one examines the prospect of its discovery one is bound to be reminded of how much that discovery will depend upon our understanding of the age we shall enter. It will be, inevitably, an age of crisis, the natural sequel to an age of turbulent confusion. Literally millions of people, of almost every nation in the world, will have to adjust themselves to a new atmosphere, strange, alarming, not seldom an atmosphere which will make claims upon them they will find it hard not to resent. After the first flush of enthusiasm over victory, it is likely to seem, it may easily remain, a sad world filled, for many, with tragic and bitter memories. Millions of refugees will go home to find their land made alien by the death and destruction it has witnessed. Others will find that a new outlook has been born which somehow does not correspond to the expectations they had formed. Not a few will discover that they cannot adjust themselves to the new world in which they have to begin anew. The scale of adaptation the world will confront is beyond anyone's power to imagine, much less to measure. Nothing we experienced in 1919 even begins to compare with the size of the issues in the post-war years.

This is more clearly the case because there is little in the literature of the inter-war period which reads like a preparation for the creation upon which we must embark. The French Revolution and the Napoleonic wars created, both in Europe and America, men of letters whose work had laid, by 1815, the foundations of a new spirit in mankind. Paine, Godwin, and Bentham in politics, Wordsworth and Coleridge, in the epoch when they still dared to dream, in poetry, Burns and Blake, were all, in England alone, building a challenge to the new society. Saint-Simon had already caught a glimpse of what would be implied, alike for good and evil, in nineteenth-century industrialism. Laplace had set the terms of a new cosmology. Goethe and Schiller had given to German literature its first decisive claim on the attention of the world; Kant and Hegel had redefined the central issues of philosophy on a basis which not a whole century of future speculation was to exhaust. Wolf in classical philology, Niebuhr in Roman history, Savigny in jurisprudence had made it abundantly clear that a new epoch had dawned in human knowledge. No one, even in the hard years of reaction after 1815, can fail to see that the outlines of a new universe had already been shaped in the womb of the old.

In the years between 1919 and 1939 it is difficult to seize that sense of a dawning renaissance. There are few figures who were able to grip the imagination of the world. There is immense achievement in science; names like those of Einstein and Dirac open new perspectives in physics. The advance in medicine and biochemistry is, proportionately, remarkable. But it is difficult to see in those twenty years any figure in philosophy or poetry, in the novel or in criticism, much less in the field of social studies, whose achievement marks a new epoch. The profusion of talent is great; and there are moments when it almost seems as though some school of thought is going to make a permanent impact on the generation. Yet I suspect that the historian will regard almost all that is likely to remain outside the realm of science and technology in the inter-war years as, at best, a silver age palely reflecting the glow of an Indian summer which fades before men feel its warmth. T. S. Eliot, Sinclair Lewis, Siegfried Sassoon, William Faulkner, all of them have either a nostalgia for the past or a strident rejection of the scene contemporary with them which means a lack of faith in themselves even when, as with T. S. Eliot, they most loudly proclaim their faith. There were philosophers of eminence like Whitehead and Bergson, Russell and Cassirer, Moore and Santayana. But it is not, I think, an exaggeration to say that their meaning was reserved for a specialized audience; they did not, like Carlyle or Mill or Ruskin in England, like Michelet or Renan in France, like Emerson or Mark Twain in America, address an audience which was almost coincident with what there was of civic-mindedness in their nations.

It is important to emphasize this contrast because it points to an element in the life of our society the consequences of which have been, I believe, more profound than we have yet begun to realize. The greatest feature of the inter-war years has been the organized externalization of pleasures, in sport, in dancing, in the cinema. That has meant the merger of the individual in the recreative mass which it is alone profitable to assemble; and this, in its turn, has meant that few people have heard any voice which cannot make its message heard by the sheer loudness of its utterance. The generation which has grown up since Versailles has lost no small part of the knowledge out of which its predecessors built their universe. It has not only undergone a massive process of secularization; it has been deeply instructed in the belief that material pleasure, taken in an external and collective way, is the clue to a modern perspective. It knows Jane Austen or Dickens as writers whose books Hollywood thought fit to film; it rarely knows them for their own sake. It has been taught to assume that an important film star, a crack aviator, a great golfer, or a famous cricketer, had a glory the splendour of which was far more real than that of the statesman or the philosopher, the scientist or the artist. Its world was a feverish, sceptical, uncertain world, in which nothing seemed fixed, in which it was thought foolish not to seize the swiftly passing joy while it lasted. All those twenty years from Versailles to the second World War have seen the rapid degeneration of a world in which reason, standards, the power to plan one's future and to enjoy the prospect of security, had been the normal lot of at any rate the class which attained to the position of rulers, into a world in which unreason was king, in which the possession of standards was obsolete Victorianism, in which there was neither the power to plan nor, often enough, even the hope of security.

We have seen something of this decline in London and New York. But to grasp its incidence in its full extent we have to think of what the experience of the inter-war years has meant to a citizen of Vienna or of Berlin, of Paris or of Rome. To anyone who had arrived at maturity before 1919 it was as though the world to which he had once possessed a chart had ceased any longer to have a pattern corresponding to the map; to anyone who grew up after 1919 it must have seemed as though the whole was a chaos incapable of reduction to order. Violence, unreason, the sudden overturn of what seemed well established, the complete inability to be sure of the shape of things to come, the growth of contempt for law, the emergence of wild passions by which men are divided as the prey from the hunter, all this has been part of the experience of these twenty years. After 1933 in Berlin, he was taught to think of Moscow as the root of all evil; from the summer of 1939 to the summer of 1941 the root of all evil became the source of eternal friendship; while on June 22, 1941, that source of friendship became again the root of evil to which he had been so painfully conditioned. One cannot say that, in the inter-war years, there was a transvaluation of all values, because that assumes the acceptance of a commonly held criterion by which the new values were measured. Rather is it true to say that the common man must have felt that the means of rational calculation had been suspended. The power of anticipating the future in which he was involved, still more, the power to assist in contributing his own experience to the making of that future seemed to grow obsolete before his very eyes. He learned, indeed, of a past in which he had these powers much as a figure in the late Victorian age must have heard his grandparents speak of the brooding sense of terror in Europe in 1848, or a twentieth-century resident of San Francisco listened to early reminiscences of the Barbary Coast after the gold rush of 1849.

No one can, I think, seriously doubt that the twenty years between the two world wars showed a rapid increase in the extent and authority of the irrational elements in society. In some degree this was evident everywhere, though their hold upon Germany after the advent of Hitler to power was beyond question their most striking manifestation. And in the increase in this irrationalism what is most important is not the emergence of an ignorant mobocracy indifferent or hostile to culture, so much as the fact that irrationalism becomes a cult which develops its gangster-leaders, and that these set out, in alliance with the traditional forces of privilege, to reduce the masses to impotence. It is difficult not to contrast the murder of Hypatia by the mob at Alexandria in the time of Synesius with the deliberate murder of Matteoti by Mussolini or with Hitler's "blood-bath" of June 30, 1934. In the pagan civilization which was then in decay, it is the masses who outrage the rule of law and the authority of the state which seeks to defend it. But in the inter-war years, it is the masses who show respect for the law, and the state-power which transforms it from a body of rational rules into a spasmodic series of tyrannical and arbitrary acts. Whereas, in the decline of Roman civilization, it was the destruction of the ruling class which invited the onset of barbarism, in the years between 1919 and 1939 it is the partnership of privilege with gangsterism which promotes the breakdown of all civilized values.

War was the inevitable outcome of an instability which men could no longer endure. But not less important than its outbreak was the question of what it would decide. It was vital in the interest of civilized living to defeat those aggressive gangsters who, whether in Berlin or Rome or Tokyo, had shown the depth of their contempt for the common man, had concerted a policy of which the central purpose was his degradation from end to instrument; they sought, in fact, to make power the test of human worth and the measure of human effort. They espoused the gospel of Success with an ardour which, since some such time as the French Revolution, no rulers of the state in any part of the civilized world had dared openly to avow. Even the Holy Alliance had been built upon a principle, even if time had deprived it of effective relevance to the problems it sought to control. But it was of the essence of the partnership of the Axis powers that they admitted the validity of no principle save the denial that any principles were valid. Their one object was to destroy all values save those which were necessary to the maintenance of their power, and, in a shifting world, it was grimly clear that the maintenance of their power depended upon a fluidity of values which deprived these of all meaning.

In this situation, it is difficult not to set the problem of victory in a context akin to that which witnessed the slow triumph of Christianity over its rivals. Now, as then, an immense distance separates the rulers from the ruled; in the inter-war years it is not unreasonable to think of the impact of Lenin and Stalin upon the traditional beneficiaries of power much as Spartacus must have seemed to that Roman aristocracy which crucified him and his followers throughout the length of the Appian Way. And the cultivated aristocrat of the decaying pagan culture must often have felt, as he listened to the crude exposition of early Christian doctrine by some zealous protagonist of the new faith, much as a sophisticated don from Oxford or Harvard must feel as he reads the passionate attacks of a Communist against the principles of the civilization to the environment of which he owes all that makes his life full and gracious. Yet even the sophisticated don may well recognize in the invective he finds so uninviting hints of a system the values of which he is prepared to accept.

And it is, I think, undeniable that, despite the general breakdown of values, our generation has a passionate yearning for some common basis of life which offers it security and the hope of happiness. That yearning has emerged with exceptional clarity in the inter-war years; it is the secret nourishment which has kept alive the spirit of man during the years of conflict. It has enabled us to bridge gulfs between nations, classes, individuals, which, a generation ago, we should have judged beyond the power of man to bridge. To take one example only: it is, I suggest, impossible to doubt that the spectacle of Russian heroism in the two years of the struggle against Hitlerism has convinced the common man, all over the world, that there was a magic in the Revolution of 1917 somehow adaptable to his own concerns. His knowledge of its meaning is small; his ability to give it institutional expression is, no doubt, still smaller. But whether it be Mr. Roosevelt or Mr. Churchill, a pilot in his Spitfire, or an ordinary private in the infantry of the North African Army, there is a sense in him that, in some way, how, perhaps, he remains uncertain, Stalingrad is the resolution of a problem for him that he must solve or die. So that he becomes anxious to find the terms upon which he is able to fit the meaning of the Russian Revolution into the traditional inheritance that is his own, American or British, French or Dutch, Belgian or Norwegian or Chinese. He even looks anxiously for the means of finding the terms upon which this coalescence of values finds a means of entry into the minds of the peoples he is fighting.

I do not, of course, mean to say that this anxiety is any more general than was the drift to the acceptance of Christianity in the period between the death of its founder and its adoption by Constantine. It is quite evident that there are those who feel about the implicit values of the Russian Revolution as bitter an antagonism as Julian the Apostate to the values of the Christian dispensation. It is quite evident, also, that the prehensility of the Russian idea varies from class to class and from country to country. My point is the different one that, in every nation, those who accept the noble formula of Aristotle that we should "strain every nerve to live in accordance with what is best in us," somehow, however obscurely, find in the Russian achievement some hint of that secret which enabled Christianity two thousand years ago to compensate for the breakdown of a world which lost its nerve in the grim years of strain after the Punic Wars and experimented with a host of esoteric religions before it finally turned to Christianity for the remaking of its values and, thereby, the recovery of a common faith which slowly made possible the restoration of security. I do not, of course, deny that in the process of experiment there were cruelty and error and persecution as there have been with ourselves. I do not even deny that men of great nobility of temper, as they look at the source of the new dispensation, are driven to something like despair by the sacrifice it involves and the price it will exact before it achieves a common acceptance.

Granted all this, I yet suggest that the basic idea of the Russian Revolution satisfies the conditions any new system of values must satisfy if it is to fill the void left by the wholesale decay of the old. It offers to the common man not only a rising standard of welfare; it enables him to see that his own productive effort is directly relevant to the standard achieved. And, as an idea, it has the immense social merit of making function and not status the basis of the individual's place in society. Men cannot, in the Russian social order, live as parasites upon the effort of others. Nor is there an individual advantage to be gained—as is the case in every other society—by the organization of scarcity; on the contrary, the organization of abundance is a benefit alike to the individual and the community. It is legitimate, therefore, to draw the inference that the Russian Revolution has ended a social order in which the wealth of a man enables him to exercise power over other men. And anyone who examines the literature of the epoch in which Christianity slowly made its way to power cannot but be moved, I think, by the contrast between the Russian attitude to the successful man and the Christian attitude to the rich man. The first is built on the recognition that the citizen's success is an addition to the well-being of the community as well as a source of benefit to himself. Whether it is the miner who hews more coal, or the engineer who discovers how to extract more power from oil, or the agricultural specialist who finds how to obtain more yield of wheat per acre, the outcome of discovery is not a threat to individual well-being. The Russian system rules out, *a priori,* that technological frustration which is endemic in any system based, like ours, upon the private ownership of the means of production.

VII

Rich and Poor in the Experience of Value-making

YET all the literature of the Christian revelation is hardly anything so much as a challenge to the rich. It is the poor who are blessed; it is the rich man who can hardly hope for entrance into the Kingdom of Heaven. There is, indeed, hardly a nation or a period in the history of the world in which the misery of the poor is not laid at the door of the rich, in which the antagonism between them is not the basis upon which the state-power is organized as a means of safeguarding the rich from attack from the poor. The heart-felt protest which Plutarch puts into the mouth of Tiberius Gracchus leads by direct tradition to Adam Smith's conception of the state as virtually a conspiracy of the rich against the poor; and the curses of the men who wrote, for example, the Book of Revelation against the imperial power of Rome differ only in the manner of their invective from the passionate denunciation of all government as illegitimate in the *Discourse on the Origins of Inequality,* which Rousseau wrote perhaps fifteen or sixteen centuries later. The problem, in short, that Christianity sought to solve was to reconcile the existence of the poverty of the poor with a state-power which safeguarded the riches of the wealthy from invasion; and, stripped of everything but essentials, it did so by promising the poor a salvation in the life to come which the rich could only achieve with difficulty. And it is significant that, after the adoption of the Church by the state, every movement in the history of the former down to the Reformation which seeks to regenerate the Church does so by the insistence that its wealth is the source of its deformation. Sects like the Beguines and the Waldenses, orders like that of Saint Francis, are built upon nothing so much as the implicit assumption that the wealth of the Church is the enemy of its divine purpose, and that by stripping itself of its temporalities it may hope to fulfil its mission upon earth.

It is, I think, in the consolation thus offered to the poor that the Church found its way, up to some such time as the Reformation, to impose its faith upon the mind of Western civilization. For the poor man who accepted its formulas it was able to proffer salvation; and it made its terms with the rich by inventing the doctrine of stewardship. Its weakness, as a theory of social life, was twofold. On the one hand, essentially, its kingdom was not of this world, its faith was therefore a scheme of values dependent upon a belief in things unseen. On the other, there were few of its votaries who could divorce themselves from a passionate and compelling interest in power in the world we know; in this regard, the dualism in the outlook of Saint Bernard, for example, who desires to combine authority over the great of this earth with devotion to the contemplation of divine things, illustrates the inherent contradiction in the Christian's outlook. He dare not seriously seek to challenge the secular state lest, in doing so, he becomes responsible for a social anarchy which is fatal to the law and order which, as Cæsar's realm, he is bidden to respect; on the other he cannot but be aware that the kingdoms of this world are, in Augustine's famous phrase, *magna latrocinia,* for which, as a Christian, he can have nothing but contempt. Up to the Reformation, the Christian salves his conscience by accepting responsibility for mitigating the lot of the poor, and, thereby, insisting to the rich that it is in their zeal for the welfare of the poor that they can find their hope of salvation.

But after the Reformation the new possibilities of production make the theory of the early and the medieval Church of decreasing applicability in those countries, especially the Protestant countries, where the new methods of production are opening the prospects of new wealth. There the psychology of the medieval Christian has a decreasing hold. Those prospects meant the need of principles of behaviour which decisively altered both the relations of Church and state, and the attitude of society to the poor. Christian theology did not meet effectively the challenge of scientific discovery; and, by some such time as the French Revolution, it had become an obligation on the citizen's part to develop his major energies to the protection or advancement of his place in secular society, and his minor energies only to attaining salvation. Or, perhaps, the change is best put by saying that the prospects of new wealth have become so alluring that the more fully a man takes advantage of them, the more certain is he to be regarded as in a state of grace. The great revival which took place after the Renaissance and the voyages of discovery was the equation of poverty with sin and the assumption that the rich man can enter the Kingdom of Heaven so long as his piety conforms to the standards exacted by the particular Church to which he belongs. The Churches therefore become in essence a part of the protective armour of the state; and it is not difficult to see why an historian like Halévy could argue that it was the Methodist revival, perhaps in conjunction with the growth of evangelicalism, which saved Great Britain from the threat of the French Revolution as, quite patently, it is the Greek Church in Russia and the Roman Catholic Church in Spain which have been in each the main safeguard of the peculiar combination of monarchy and reactionary privilege.

But by becoming, slowly after the Reformation, and swiftly after the French Revolution, in essence a part of the protective armour of the state, the Church has paid a heavy price for its alliance. What it lost in increasing measure was the faith of the poor in the principles it urged. The elements which contributed to the growing secularization of society are, no doubt, both many and difficult to disentangle in their due proportions. What is at any rate certain is that from the French Revolution onward the decay of religious faith, especially among the poor, in Western civilization is widespread and rapid and decisive. Partly, it is the impact of science on the modern mind, not least of historical science; the moment that the principles of Christian theology are tested by the normal canons of evidence, the power of the Church to justify a social order of which both the irrationality and the injustice are growingly clear was bound in the nature of things to decline. Organized religion then increasingly became either one form among many of social conformity, or based, as with the Society of Friends, upon the possession of an esoteric conviction which, because it was essentially mystical in character, had no power to convey objective proofs to any who did not happen to share the mystical insight of the particular Church or believer.

And all this meant that, in the nineteenth century, with growing force, the place taken by religious creeds in the earlier epochs of Western civilization was taken by political creeds. Power in its secular form no doubt continued to pay to religious faith the homage of official reverence; but it was, for the most part, a formal etiquette by which relatively few were deceived. The effect of the decay in religious faith was increasingly to transfer the centre of importance from the after life to this world; and this meant that the scheme of values which bound men together in any community had to give proof that it enabled fulfilment, and not frustration, to take place in this world. That is the explanation of the rise of socialism; it was, above all, a philosophy of values relevant to the individual's self-realization in the only life about which we can speak with confidence and conviction. And the effect of the rise of socialism was that, almost everywhere, either men of property joined in a coalition to prevent its advance, or they sought the means of offering to its votaries enough of concession to prevent the principles of socialism from becoming the main line of division between parties and classes.

On the whole, that coalition was successful until some such time as the outbreak of the first World War. Its result was to set the philosophy of *bourgeois* civilization in a light of decreasing strength. For, first, it became obvious that the new world could no longer come to the release of the old; the problems of America and Canada and Australia were as difficult of resolution as those of Europe. And, in the second place, it became clear that the productive relations of *bourgeois* society could not take advantage of the technological possibilities of scientific discovery; the consequence of this fact was that the *bourgeois* system of values was no longer able to satisfy the established expectations of the masses. Wholesale unemployment became a world phenomenon; and with it there evolved an intellectual outlook which was either sceptical of the values which, in the nineteenth century, had enabled the men of property to maintain their hold, or which quite frankly denied the adequacy of those values. Nor was it possible for the Churches to recover the ground they had lost in the course of the previous century. The task which had been performed by men like Wesley or Chateaubriand for millions was now effective only for a handful who were themselves, like Mr. T. S. Eliot, wedded to a dream which had already faded when they dreamed it.

No doubt the tradition of the past was strong; and there were many, even among the masses themselves, who hardly dared to question its right to acceptance. There were many more who, when it was reformulated by Hitler or Mussolini in terms with which they were familiar, were ready to believe that a change in form was a change in substance. But, at bottom, the real fact was the breakdown of the synthesis which had meant so long an epoch of peace until 1914, the rise of a challenge to the foundations upon which it rested, the growing dissatisfaction with all the values it imposed. Not even the immensity of the triumph of the capitalist democracies in 1918 could give a new glamour to the synthesis; after a moment's rejoicing in the victory over Germany, there re-emerged the mood of dissatisfaction and discontent. It is, I think, true to say that in the inter-war years there are two phenomena of vital importance. The first is the sense, by which all men of substance are troubled, that the Russian Revolution is, in its basic idea, as profound a challenge to their authority as they had encountered since the Reformation. The second is their growing willingness to accept as their defenders the outlaws of civilization to whom reason and orderly progress are devoid of meaning, and even dangerous. The fact that Mr. Churchill, whose pride in the imperial tradition of England had made him suspect almost from the outset the danger to that tradition which Hitler symbolized, was yet prepared enthusiastically to support General Franco, is evidence enough that much of the historic state-wisdom upon which the effectiveness of the synthesis depends was in process of rapid erosion.

Our problem is the simple but vital one of finding a new system of values which enables men to live together in peace; for the civilized tradition, as Whitehead has so eloquently insisted, means nothing so much as the movement from force to persuasion. The power of any supernatural religion to build that tradition has gone; the deposit of scientific inquiry since Descartes has been fatal to its authority. It is therefore difficult to see upon what basis the civilized tradition can be rebuilt save that upon which the idea of the Russian Revolution is founded. It corresponds, its supernatural basis apart, pretty exactly to the mental climate in which Christianity became the official religion of the West. For, on the one hand, it satisfies the masses by its power to offer to them a sense of individual fulfilment now wholly unattainable within the confines of any alternative social system. And, on the other, it offers to the *élite* a vocation of leadership which seems likely to replace with real adequacy that wealth so often unrelated to function which has done so much to discredit the claims of privilege in our time. Wherever the idea of the Russian Revolution has taken hold it has bred in its exponents a yearning for spiritual salvation; and it is out of that yearning that there is at least the hope that we may recover a philosophy of values.

I think this hope is real even though, in its actual expression, the Russian idea, like early Christianity, is encountered in many forms of which the ugliness is undeniable. Its votaries, like the early Christians, are often brutal and cruel; like the early Christians, too, they have a deep and irritating sense of moral superiority over those who have not been able to accept the validity of their insight. They cause confusion and disorder by the vigour with which they press their claims. They create indignation by the contempt they pour on ceremonies and habits which an older tradition of value had rendered precious to those who perform them. They make their rivals angry because they so often seem to operate at two levels of morality, one for themselves and one for those who do not feel able to share their faith. The vigour with which they challenge the older dispensations has often about it as ungracious and fierce an invective as Tertullian poured out upon those who stayed in the ancient ways. They treat disagreement as a form, even a dangerous form, of sin with something of the passion which early Christian literature displays. And in their selfless power of sacrifice there is hidden a lust for victory which makes us understand why a man like Augustine could pursue Donatus with a passion that it is difficult not to term malignant. They are even the objects of the same ugly persecution as that which was visited upon the Christians before the final decision of Constantine. There are even attributed to the Russian idea the same mythological enormities as led to the imposition of something like outlawry upon those of its adherents whom its enemies could discover. The orthodox narrative of the early Russian experiment reads like nothing so much as the early pagan accounts of the first Christian communities.

Yet the hope is real, even though the idea of the Russian Revolution, in its multiform expressions, seems to come hardly less to destroy than to fulfil. And the reason for the reality of the hope is that it offers, as no rival offers, a way out for the common man from the bitter frustration of our time. It has insisted upon his inherent dignity as a person. It has given to manual labour a higher status than it has ever elsewhere attained. It has refused to accept that separation of manual labour from the cultural heritage which has, with rare individual exceptions like Spinoza, characterized all past civilizations. It has refused to allow the possession of wealth without function; the *élite* brought to power by the Russian Revolution has been able to disregard wealth or birth, race or creed. It has found the means of giving to a larger proportion of its working population a significance which arises out of the duties allotted to it than any comparable experiment has so far achieved. It has opened more widely a career to the talents than any previous regime; and the career so opened has had a direct relevance to the public good. It is not surprising that, even when all the blunders and follies of its rulers are taken into account, the ethos of the Russian Revolution should have built, as early Christianity built, the elements of a universal fellowship. In no other country in the world today has there grown up an exhilaration more profound, a will to self-sacrifice so inherently compelling. Faith in the Revolution possesses for its devotees the same kind of magic hold as Christianity exercised over its first followers. It is a call to what is highest in man, and a call to the fulfilment of what is highest not merely as an offering upon the altar of self, as the promotion of a private interest, but as a contribution to a fellowship in which selfhood is fulfilled in the context of a greater purpose by which it is absorbed.

I do not, of course, deny that the idea is as partial, as fragmentary, and as interstitial as was the Christian idea in its early days. Just as the latter had often to speak in accents, to utilize a doctrine, suited to a multitude that was often ignorant, and not seldom hostile, to its claims, so has it been true of the Russian Revolution that the gap between, say, the dream that Lenin dreamed and the actuality has been profound. That has not, I submit, made the significance of the Russian Revolution any less; the gap between the faith of the Gospels and the achievement of the Church did not make the transition from paganism to Christianity anything less than a recovery of nerve in civilization, a move from decay to regeneration, a revival of the values that give to man his status as *Homo sapiens.* No doubt as the revolutionary idea has established itself, it has involved in those whom it has influenced cruelty and cowardice, dishonesty and disorder. These are part of the price a society is bound to pay which attempts the transvaluation of all values. The real point is that the faith the idea represents has cut more deeply into human thought than any rival faith; more, that as it has found fulfilment it has created a greater volume and a more intense volume of hope than any series of events in the modern history of mankind.

What it is urgent, therefore, for us to understand is that the Russian revolutionary idea meets the two supreme tests which any faith must be able to meet which hopes to achieve a regeneration of civilized values. It must be a source of strength in adversity to those who accept it; and it must seem not less vital after it has gone well on the way of its regenerating mission than it did when it was able to attract a poor handful of brave acolytes. I suggest that, with all its limitations, the Russian Revolution meets both of those conditions. Its informing idea has been adapted both to success and failure. It has evoked a religion of service to the community which has elevated the men and women who compose it. It possesses that magic power which, with most of us, only great danger has seemed able to evoke, the power of living to an end greater than a merely private end. In this aspect, the revolutionary generation in Russia has had the exciting quality we associate with the fifth century B.C. in Athens, or the Elizabethan age. Year in and year out of its history, men and women, both young and old, have found in it the inspiration which made them feel that they were a part, however small, of the great world-purpose which has the future on its side. And that inspiration has affected not merely the great man, the powerful man, the citizen of representative capacity. It has touched the humblest, too, the clerk in a department store, the man who cleans the streets, even, as the great experiment of Bolshevo has made evident, the criminal in his prison. It has created the conviction that to work for the good of humanity, to take even a small step towards freeing it from its chains, is infinitely worth while. It is the existence of that conviction in so large a proportion of Russian citizens that has made it impossible for anyone in our generation to be indifferent to the outcome of the Russian experiment. Friendly or hostile, we have all known that its results, one way or another, would change the history of the world.

There is one point here upon which I must comment because it has so often misled men in their judgment of the Russian achievement. "You claim for its reforming idea," it is said, "a basis upon which there can be a regeneration of our values, the revival of a faith which compensates humanity for the lost generation and two world wars. But if one examines the history of the Russian Revolution the scale of individual achievement is disappointing. There are no scientists of the first order; if the literature is interesting, there is no Tolstoy, no Dostoevski, no Chekhov, no Pushkin; there is one composer only whose music has aroused a general interest; there is little of interest in what has been written on social matters; outside the film, and perhaps the theatre, the revolutionary idea of which you speak so highly has added nothing to our heritage which, ten years from now, the world will care to remember."

It is important to deal with the issue raised by this argument. It is important, first, to remember that the main energies of Russia have been devoted in the first generation of its revolutionary history to the sheer struggle for survival. It is rare, under such conditions, for science or literature, art or music, to be produced that is not practically relevant to that survival. Hardly before the time of Andrew Jackson did an America which was struggling to subdue its vast wilderness enter into the culture of the world; and none of the British Dominions, despite their assurance of physical safety, has made any outstanding contribution to science or art. The essential Russian achievement in this first generation has been to make its people literate, to confer upon them faith in their destiny, and to organize them against the danger of attack from without, which, had it succeeded, would have made the forces of counter-revolution the masters of the world. The contribution of revolutionary Russia has been, first, the transformation of an illiterate peasant community into a modern economy in which the necessary forces of industrialization, human and mechanical, have been organized; its contribution, in the second place, has been the demonstration that the backward peoples can be brought into the civilized foreground; and, in the third place, its contribution can be summarized in the epic feat of Stalingrad. What Russia is to do for the cultural heritage of mankind we cannot expect to know until, on the international plane, it has access to security, and draws therefrom the inference that its people may enjoy the physical and spiritual conditions which evoke creative utterance in the arts and science. Those conditions are rarely available when, as from 1917, the very existence of the experiment is in doubt. In years such as those the mind of a nation is bound up with the daily task the experiment requires to be fulfilled. It is only when a nation passes from the fever of acute danger to the temperature which leaves the creative mind at ease that one can fairly look for achievement to which only freedom of mind and heart can give birth. That freedom, so far, it has not fallen to the lot of revolutionary Russia to enjoy.

My argument is, I think, reinforced by another consideration. Russian socialism since 1917 has been, for the most part, a doctrine on the defence against the world much as Christianity was on the defence in the first three centuries of its history. And, after all, after the first supreme expression of its faith in the Gospels, there is no Christian literature that has much more than an historical importance until the work of Saint Augustine. A movement which most of the world agrees to shun, because most of the world wishes to reject the values it seeks to establish, tends in the nature of things to polemic rather than to art. I do not mean to suggest that the two are incompatible; but I suspect that most writers whose work is set in the context of the narrow perspective polemic is likely to enforce lack the elbow-room they need for great creation. The *Confessions* and the *City of God* are great literature because in them Augustine was unburdening all his heart to the world in a way he could not even attempt when his task was the more narrow one of proving to his contemporaries that the views of the Donatists were an evil heresy. Since 1917, the major part of Russian literary work has been comparable with the controversial treatises of Augustine for the simple reason that its purpose has been not to amuse or to delight, not, even, to write for the pleasure of self-liberation, but to establish a doctrine in the minds of its citizens as truth against which long centuries of past experience were an argument and a protest.

VIII

The Soviet Idea and Its Perspectives

WE HAVE to remember, as we examine the postulates of the Revolution, that it came to a land staggering under defeat, grim with poverty, and, after the fall of Tsarism, racked for almost five years by ruthless civil war. It is the very fact that the Russian people, after eight years of agony, not only embarked on the immense experiment which has changed the perspective of world-history, but built out of the experiment, of which the inmost essence was sacrifice, a power which enabled them to hold and defeat a great army which had swept over Europe, which ought to make us conscious that an idea capable of these results is vital to the future of mankind. When the last word has been said against Russian bureaucracy, against the hindrances to the political self-expression we know in Britain and the United States, against the scale upon which its terror has been conducted, against the ugly Byzantinism of its party infallibility, the solemn truth remains that in the Soviet Union, since the October Revolution, more men and women have had more opportunity of self-fulfilment than anywhere else in the world. The experiment, no doubt, has been hard, ruthless, at times even brutal. We have got to make up our minds, nevertheless, to two things. First, if it had been an experiment such as it was conducted by tender-minded men, it would not have had even the remotest prospect of endurance; quite certainly, it would have been broken in pieces by its enemies within and its enemies without. And, second, of all the nations united to drive back the tide of counter-revolution, it is the only one which, after the victory has been won, knows without doubt that its people move to the control of their own destiny. For in no other nation is it implicit in the productive relations that have been established that an advance in economic well-being accrues to the whole people and not to a part of the people. Even though it still be true that the Russian standard of life compares unfavourably with that of Britain and Holland in Europe, or of the United States on the American continent, its economic system is differentiated from all of these by the fact that its central principle is that of expansion for all, and that it is undominated, even uninfluenced, by any interest which can seek wealth or welfare through the technique of restriction. Granted the scale of its resources, and granted, also, the prospect of an enduring peace, on the experience of the Russian Revolution since 1917, it is the logical implication of that differentiation it owes to Lenin and his successors that its people have the right to a hope which, in the end, outdistances that of any other people. It is urgent to bear in mind that hope is the source of faith, and that it is faith which gives to the members of a society the values which enable them to hold the great ends of life in common.

If, therefore, it be accepted that our own time bears a profound resemblance to the era in which Christianity was born, it seems to me that we are entitled to conclude that the regeneration of values which the new faith effected after, no doubt, a long and bitter struggle, is more likely to be secured in our own age by the central idea of the Russian Revolution than by any alternative principle we are in a position to choose. The achievement of Christianity was to persuade the poor to accept their poverty in part by the promise of salvation and, in part also, by imposing upon the rich an obligation to mitigate by charity the miseries of the poor in this world. There is an important sense in which that achievement was a necessary condition of the process of civilization. For, first of all, without it there would have been, in the decline of Rome, no hope of anything but anarchy since there would have been no rational foundation for power. If we agree that values can exist only in a cosmos, that, without them, society is, as it were, in a permanent state of siege, Christianity convinced the masses that they could accept without undue repining the traditional social order in Europe and even, in considerable degree, effected for them a diminution of its acerbities. And this was probably a necessary function in a period when man's control over the forces of nature involved, in the nature of things, an inescapable poverty for the masses. Christianity rationalized a scheme of values which meant a considerable reinforcement of the power to maintain peaceful social relations by setting the idea of poverty in the context of salvation. Its contempt for the things of this world, its projection of all that made life important into the Kingdom of Heaven made this world endurable for those who accepted its principles. By making this world endurable it accomplished the important mission of transforming a power which would otherwise have seemed irrational coercion into a type of authority which was not only blessed by God but, also, *sub specie aeternitatis,* of relative unimportance. There seemed little need for a Spartacus to organize the poor to rebel against injustice if this world was no more than a vestibule to that eternal life in which it was the poor who entered into possession of the Kingdom of Heaven.

This rationalization is intelligible enough until the sixteenth century. With the Renaissance, the voyages of discovery, the Reformation, the scientific revolution accomplished by Copernicus and Kepler, by Galileo and Newton, and the overthrow of the scholastic philosophy by Descartes, the growth, alongside or because of these, of new and immense economic opportunities, not least, of opportunities opened to men who, formerly, had little chance of realizing them, the validity of the Christian generalization began to fade as a means of justifying a system of values. It began to fade, in large degree, because the economic system which had made its acceptance intelligible enough began to undergo fundamental changes. It is as good a Puritan as Baxter who emphasizes the importance of the utilitarian principle: "Knowledge," he wrote, "is to be valued according to its usefulness." [1] That outlook must be set over against the contempt for science that we find in the early Fathers of the Church

---

[1] Richard Baxter, *Christian Directory* (ed. of 1825), Vol. I, p. 13.

so that it even became regarded as a partnership with the Devil. The great change is the slow liberation of knowledge from dependence upon authority; from a period in which, as in the early days of the Royal Society, science is held to be a means of discovering the glory of God, we pass from Thomas Sprat's explicit renunciation of monastic asceticism as incompatible with the frame of mind which "makes us serviceable to the world," [1] through an accommodation, as with Sydenham and Boyle, between religion and science, even between Puritanism and science, to the situation where, as Locke is never tired of insisting, that knowledge only should be pursued "as may be of use to us." By the time that, in the last third of the seventeenth century, the idea of progress has come to maturity, it is the sense of science as the key to that power which will unlock the hidden riches of the universe which is the predominant temper of the investigator. By the time of the French Encyclopædia religion and science have developed that mutual hostility which they have never since lost. Thenceforward, wealth and power have become so closely related that the rationalization of early Christianity rapidly ceases to be the effective sanction of a scheme of values in this world.

For as scientific progress subdues nature to the purposes of man, the idea of the heavenly city of early Christianity gives way to the dream in which the reward of man's effort is not salvation in the life to come but happiness upon this earth itself. And so long as the expansion of well-being continues, the scheme of values upon which the security of civilization depends maintains its hold upon mankind. It is, of course, subject to an occasional challenge; it may even raise doubts in the minds of men who, like Matthew Arnold, accept in general the benefits it confers. It is not until the war of 1914–18 that men begin to realize, on any serious scale, how fragile is the basis upon which the security of that civilization rests. It is when they begin to realize that, within the accepted conventions of the law, above all in the productive relations it sanctions, there is no such thing

[1] *History of the Royal Society*, pp. 305–306.

as inevitable progress, that there is no chance therein of permanently satisfying the established expectations of the masses, that the need of a new scheme of values begins to be clear. And as the need becomes clear, there emerges also the understanding that a price must be paid for its attainment. Values are born, in fact, of the ability to satisfy mass-demands; they wither away as that ability diminishes.

In the inter-war years most of us have been conscious that this ability was decreasing, and our consciousness was sharpened by the knowledge that its decrease was set in an environment which offered greater possibilities of satisfaction than at any previous time. This is the reason for the cynicism and disillusion which have marked this period. We have felt our chains to be a heavier burden because we have suspected increasingly that there was an ever lesser need to bear them. And the second World War has given this mood a definition more sharp and arresting than even the inter-war years displayed. It has done so because it has registered so massively and in so many directions the failure of our scheme of values. For despite all its ugliness and tragedy, it has demonstrated beyond dispute the contradictions which lie at the heart of contemporary civilization. It makes the unemployed man an immediate source of social value. It compels us to transcend those relations of production which were, until almost the day of its outbreak, a barrier in the path of useful effort. It has given not merely significance, but also the chance of heroism, to scores of thousands who, until the hour of danger, led lives which hardly had meaning even for themselves. It has taught millions of us, all over the world, how much we could do without, which we had previously insisted made possible the fulfilment of our natures. It has shown the hollowness of concepts like sovereignty and neutrality which lingered on into an age where they were technically outmoded. Above all, perhaps, it has decisively exhibited the futility of an individualistic scheme of social organization which refused to freedom that social context, both national and international, from which alone it can derive a creative meaning.

The way in which the second World War has revealed the breakdown of our scheme of values permits, indeed, of endless illustration. But I doubt whether any aspect of its revelation is more decisive or more complete than the way in which it has altered for all men of goodwill the significance of the Russian Revolution. Men who before the Russian armies had held up the grim advance of Hitler and his legions were as certain of nothing as of their hatred for the great legacy of Lenin and his successors now find without effort in its ideology the basis upon which a permanent friendship can be based. It is admitted, indeed, by all who have a mind still capable of learning, that the civilization of Western Europe and America has got, somehow, to fit the basic principles of Lenin's analysis of our time into its pattern. They may admit it with anguish or reluctance. What is important is the fact that they are driven to admit it in much the same kind of way as the Roman citizen of Constantine's age admitted the basic principles of Christianity into the pattern of his thought. The Communist who yesterday was an outlaw is today a partner in our purposes; and we have had no difficulty in admitting that the partnership alters in a decisive way the manner in which we regard the world about us.

IX

The Soviet Idea and Victory

GIVEN the fact of victory by the United Nations, it seems to me inescapable that the Russian idea will play the same part as the principles of 1789 in reconstituting the outlook of the next age. Unless we claim that the Churches will renew their hold on men's allegiance—and there is no serious evidence for the validity of such a claim—the Russian idea seems likely to be the pivotal source from which all values will find the means of renewal. I do not, of course, argue for one moment that the acceptance of the idea will be either simple or straightforward; the history of Christianity itself, the history, too, of the impact of the French Revolution upon the last century and a half, is a sufficient warning against the notion of such ease. There is nothing to which men are so toughly resistant as the acceptance of a new idea, and that the more certainly when it so clearly involves a drastic change in their social habits. It is not difficult to believe that states like Poland or institutions like the Roman Catholic Church will adjust themselves only with painful slowness to the thesis of the Russian Revolution, just as, to take another example, British statesmen have only adjusted their minds with painful slowness to the idea of a free United States or a free Ireland or a free India. The Græco-Roman culture for long regarded the claims of Christianity as nothing so much as an undermining of values of which the superiority was manifest; even Gibbon could write of its victory as "the triumph of barbarism and religion."

But the Roman Empire perished, and the Christian Church remained because the latter developed what the former lost, a creative power which enabled it to satisfy the demands that it encountered. Even through the Dark Ages it kept alight a flame which slowly developed into a fire comparable both in its power to warm the heart and light the mind of man with the culture that it superseded. My point is the vital one that, in the conditions we confront, the principles of the Russian Revolution have a similar function to perform. They have the mysterious power of renovating values, of renewing the faith of man in himself, at a time when the dark shadows seem, otherwise, likely to close about him. They have that power because of their ability to inspire hope, and so to enable him to meet the challenge of a time when his philosophy no longer satisfies his needs. It is irrelevant, on this view, that there is in these principles much that will require massive adaptations to special environments before they become acceptable. We should no more expect an experiment which regenerated corrupt and half-barbaric Russia to become a living faith unchanged in Britain or the United States than we should expect Christianity to function without change in Rome or Madrid or London. What is important is the different issue of whether the central ethos round which those principles are built have the kind of universal power the early Christian Church developed to renovate the values of our civilization by awakening a new inspiration in the men whose lives have to be guided by values that are quick and creative, instead of dying or in decay.

It may be said that the analogy does not hold for the sufficient reason that the victory of the United Nations itself constitutes an effective renovation. I do not myself see how any serious observer can accept this view. For, in the first place, the United Nations won an overwhelming triumph in 1918, and the decay of values we are witnessing followed directly upon the triumph. And, in the second place, no victory is itself a guarantee that the values will be renewed. That is bound to depend upon the use to which it is put, the principles by which it is informed. There is no knowledge, as yet, either of that future use or of those future principles. If it be said that we have the solemn commitment of the Atlantic Charter, and the programme President Roosevelt so eloquently summarized in the Four Freedoms, it is important to remember the fate which attended the Fourteen Points of President Wilson. And the very fact that this war has penetrated so much more deeply into our lives than the last war may easily have the grim result of making the power of reason of less authority at its close than was the case in 1918. It may be true that, in the hour of danger, we all insist upon the life of virtue we shall lead when we come again to safety. But experience suggests that, when safety has in fact been given to us, we forget without difficulty the pledges we have made, or give to them an interpretation which makes them unrecognizable to those who acted on the assumption that we meant what we said.

That, after all, has been not only the history of Christianity itself; it has also been the characteristic of all revolutions. The Apostolic age sought to make a great fellowship of men and women the values in whose lives transcended the distortions of a society in which the privileges of a few involved the inherent frustration of the lives of the many. No one can read the simple majesty of those first historic records without the sense that they were moved by a faith in equality and fraternity which gave them a freedom rivalled only in the rarest moments of subsequent history. But once the Church seeks alliance with, and is adopted by, the state, the freshness and simplicity of its vision seem to disappear. So it was with the Reformation and the English civil wars; so it was, also, in 1789 and 1848. The dream does not maintain its splendour in the reality.

If we ask why this should be the case, the answer, no doubt, is a complicated one. Partly, it lies in the fact of the human constitution itself, its inability to exercise power without abusing it. Partly, the explanation is historical; no social change, however great, can efface the traces of the behaviour conditioned by the situation it is seeking to destroy. Partly, again, no new system of values is likely in every area in which it operates to possess the same validity; even in a small body like the Society of Friends the relations of Fox and Nayler make it clear that men eager to work together see the same principles in a different perspective even when they are convinced that they must not fail to co-operate.

Our problem will be of a specially intense kind because the foundations of the new values towards which we shall move is more likely to be negative than positive, to be born of a community of hatred rather than from a partnership of affection. We are likely, at least in the first instance, to know what we have united to destroy rather than be certain what we are united to build. And that may easily mean, unless we are very careful, that, on the morrow of victory, what will impress us is as much the languor of the masses as their authority. They will have overthrown the counter-revolution without being either clear or confident what they have overthrown it for. As the early Christian emperors performed the rites of their faith, while so often denying the end those rites were to serve, so, after the defeat of Hitlerism and its allies, there is a grave danger that both the masses and their leaders will speak with passion the language of that freedom and democracy for which they have fought so bravely without possessing the energy, perhaps even the desire, to translate the language into the deed.

No one, certainly, who lived through the war of 1914–18 will under-estimate the danger that men may confound the exhilaration of victory with the achievement of a new social philosophy. In considerable measure, that was the disease which afflicted Christianity after its adoption by the Empire. As we examine the breakdown of our culture, it is against precisely this disease that we have to take precautions. For hardly any tragedy would be more grim than to expend so immense an effort on a new start, only to find that we are travelling again upon the road we thought we had abandoned. And the probability of this confusion is more real than we like to admit. It did not make very much difference to a medieval serf whether he spent his days in bondage to some secular lord or to the abbot of some great monastery. It will not help us much to have defeated Hitlerism unless, with its defeat, we abandon altogether the values which Hitlerism has sought to impose. No mood will be more sterile, as we begin the task of reconstruction, than one in which the main feature is the mere adoption of new names for things we had hoped to end. To discover the safeguard against the advent of that mood is one of the supreme tasks before us at the present time.

My own view is that the safeguard is available to us on the condition that we have the courage to use it. It lies in the determination to discover the reality of the individual and to offer him the means of being significant in a world the very size and complexity of which tends to destroy his personality. Here, once again, the analogy between the early period of Christianity and the idea of the Russian Revolution is important. The great virtue of the early Christian Church lay in its emphasis on the elevation of the common man. It offered to the humblest of its believers the right to a faith in his salvation. It rejected the narrow nationalism of the creed from which it diverged to propagate a universalism which made the identities of men infinitely more important than their differences. The black slave in Alexandria had, once he had this faith, a secret source of nourishment which made his inner life more real and far more happy than anything he endured at the hands of a pagan master who exerted over him the power of life and death. The very fact, indeed, that he might die in the arena for the God he worshipped assured him a salvation in which he saw all things in a new light and at a different valuation.

It was the victory of this idea of an assured salvation, won slowly and painfully over long years of struggle, which gave a new status to the personality of the common man. In the twenty centuries which have followed its formulation there have, of course, been ebb and flow, both loss and gain. But I think it is an accurate historical generalization to say that, from the Reformation onward, the drive to a recognition of the common man's claim is as persistent as it is widespread. Even when its basis in the supernatural begins to fade, the claim is not less determined. It is fostered by the discovery of America. It feeds on the growth of a challenge by the middle class to aristocratic predominance.

The events of the French Revolution take it forward in a vast stride to a plane that a slave in Rome or a medieval serf would hardly have recognized. To deny the reality of this growth in the power of man to affirm his own essence, to find, as it were, the terms of his power of self-fulfilment, cannot be seriously justified. Hope grew larger in the four hundred years from 1500 because the mastery of nature by man offered to it larger prospects than it had previously known.

But one begins to detect, in the first years of the twentieth century, a shadow across that hope. The expansion begins to slow down. There seems to be a note of stridency in the answer to men's claims. The external relations of states display an increasing hint of urgent danger; and in their internal relations the suspicion begins to grow that the challenge to tradition is passing legitimate bounds. The general emergence, especially in Germany and Japan, of a politics of power, in which the test of good is success, and the citizen a means to an end he does not share in defining, grows more evident year by year. What seems to have happened is that by 1914 the relations of production made impossible the satisfaction of expanding claims. And to the men who held in every state the reins of power the notion that those relations could undergo any fundamental alteration seemed a fantastic one, the dreams, they said, of the unsuccessful, who sought to achieve by the law what their capacity did not permit them to accomplish. Most of the men who had those dreams were either rather pitiful exiles, like Marx, or prophets who, like William Morris, had the unpractical idealism of the man with poetic insight. So that when the system broke down in 1914, those who were responsible for its reconstruction four years later did not, outside of Russia, even conceive that it could be planned on new principles. On the contrary, they treated Lenin and his colleagues, who had the audacity to take power in the name of the people, as the enemies of mankind; and it was their first concern to remake the civilization which had foundered as near in design to the old as they could dare. The result was the inevitable one that though the leaders of the vanquished nations were overthrown, no real effort was made to change those relations of production, or the institutions which, like the sovereign state, they rendered necessary, out of which the war of 1914 had developed. The real outcome of the first World War was the second World War; for in the intervening years there was no statesman in power, outside of Russia, to whom a frontal attack on vested interests appeared permissible.

In its absence, the mental climate of moral disillusion and economic collapse was unavoidable. Men had the sense everywhere that the youth of the world had been sent to die for a dream which the vested interests of the world prevented from fulfilment. So that there developed a *malaise* which seemed to most either to deprive the cosmic drama of a rational meaning or to interpret it in terms of innumerable mysticisms into the categories of which what William James called the "irreducible brute facts" would rarely fit without the assistance of symbols and allegories so massive that the reconciliation of faith and the event was hardly possible to any thinking mind. It became each year more obvious that the plan of salvation which the Christian Churches had erected on the ruins of the Græco-Roman culture no longer worked. We had the means to greater wealth and greater power than in any previous age; yet there had been grimly reborn that sense of frustration and failure which had led to the breakdown of Roman civilization. And from that sense, above all among the privileged classes, there was born anew that mood of fear which has always led an aristocracy, as it led the Romans in their treatment of Spartacus and his followers, to replace the magnanimity which it feels to be the price of its position, when it is secure, by a fiendish cruelty which is nothing so much as an effort to still the doubts of the masses. For it is those doubts which undermine the faith upon which the security of a ruling class is built. Either the conditions of its renovation must be found, or a new system of values will be sought for by those to whom the old no longer brings fulfilment.

What has become obvious in our generation is that within the postulates of our present economic system there is no hope of finding the conditions of renovation; that is why the ruling classes of Italy and Germany called in the gangsters to destroy the democratic principle, why, also, Japanese security became dependent upon militarist expansion. But it is important to realize that Hitler and Mussolini and the Japanese militarists are, together with their satellites, merely the end-terms in a series which directly influences the manner of life of us who fight them. For it has not been easy for the privileged classes of Britain and America to recognize until almost the twelfth hour had struck that Fascism in its various forms was nothing so much as a denial of the rights of personality. They were afraid that a trial of strength with Fascism would let loose those forces of revolution which denied their claim to a privileged position; that was why the men of Vichy France preferred surrender to a freedom which would have involved the remaking of a democratic dynamic which is by its nature incompatible with privilege. That is why, also, though we fight in partnership with Russia, are able, in full measure, to admire the courage of its people, there is never long absent from the minds of our rulers, both here and in the United States, a certain scepticism about our capacity to find a basis upon which we and the Russians can reach a permanent understanding. Our rulers, truth to tell, are more at their ease with men like Franco or Salazar than they have been, so far, with men like Lenin or Stalin. Nor is it without significance that there were days when Munich seemed a triumph to Mr. Chamberlain and the main part of his supporters.

Our lack of ease with the Russian leaders is strangely comparable with that lack of ease with the makers of the French Revolution which led Edmund Burke to become the spokesman of romantic conservatism a century and a half ago. We have that lack of ease because the Russian leaders have begun a renovation of values among their people comparable to that of France in 1789. They have set on foot a revolutionary remaking of power which has already begun to affect both the human spirit and social institutions with something like the force of the

Christian revelation two thousand years ago. It is, of course, like all supreme turning points in the history of thought, a refashioning of the modes of human behaviour. It has called for adjustments to which our historic political categories are hardly applicable. Above all, it has destroyed among the Russian people the scheme of values which we had associated with their governance; even more, we are not yet certain that it is not a challenge to our own. So that in the twenty-five years that have passed since the October Revolution, our main analysis of Russian events has sought to emphasize not the new values which are in the making there, but the price which has been paid—and it is, of course, a heavy price—by those who have opposed the making of those values. We have dealt with the Russian Revolution much as the Roman Empire from Nero to Diocletian dealt with the Christian Church, as though it was a mixture of blasphemy and conspiracy. We have done so because, being unwilling to recognize that, within the ancient framework, the possibility of progress was exhausted, we could not accept the validity of the structure the Russians had begun to erect without admitting that our own was in fact open to challenge. We were aware that a new world-outlook was in the making in Russia; but we could not come to terms with it unless we recognized how profound were the changes we must accept in our own philosophy of value.

It is this refusal to come to terms with the Russian faith that is perhaps the source of the greatest danger we confront today on the moral plane. For while it is true that she shall be vouchsafed the crowning mercy of victory over Hitlerism, we shall, in all likelihood, attain it without inquiring into the uses to which that victory will be put. And this means that once again, as in 1918, while we overthrow our rival, we do not discover the necessary conditions of abiding peace. We stand in the grave peril of men who mistake courage for ideas. No one who has seen Britain in these grim years of battle will doubt the courage for a moment; perhaps never in our history has it been more widespread or more intense. But the display of courage is not enough. It is the vestibule to a philosophy; it is not itself a philosophy. There still remains the issue, when the enemy has been overthrown, of finding a faith which elicits in time of peace the spirit which gave most Englishmen, during the Battle of Britain, the sense that they were truly soldiers in the war of human liberation.

The problem of maintaining that spirit is the central problem we shall face at the close of the war. On the evidence we have, we are, I think, entitled to conclude that the capacity required for its evocation is there. Stalingrad, Dunkirk, El Alamein, the Bataan Peninsula, these are, after all, only supreme hours in an epic struggle in which, if the human spirit has at moments seemed near exhaustion, it has always, as if strengthened by the depth of danger, found new power when it was wanted. But if there is one lesson implicit in this experience, it is the lesson which the early Christian and the Communist alike have taught the world—that at a time when a civilization is in decay it requires a profound faith to revitalize the values that are the secret of its strength. And it is in the highest degree unlikely that a profound faith can be born of any system in which, as in our own, not only is there a divorce between privilege and function, but also the relations of production prevent the satisfaction in the masses of the expectations they have come to regard as legitimately founded. It has become true of our time, as it was true of that *ancien régime* which not even the genius of Turgot could reform, that, as he put it, "the laws have everywhere favoured that inequality of fortunes which corrupts a certain number that the rest may be doomed to degradation and misery." The Christian faith, in its period of power, overcame this consequence by offering to the common man the secret consolation of heaven. But now that the basis upon which that faith was built has crumbled before critical examination, neither the Churches nor any other religious organizations can hope to effect the work of renovation.

X

The Source of New Values

OUR source must be discovered in the world about us: that is the urgent lesson of the period since, above all, the French Revolution. And if we are to cope seriously with our problem, we must admit that there is no answer to it save in our power to recreate the climate of hope and eagerness among ordinary people. That climate, when the immediate danger is over, will not come from some petty experiment here or there; it will come only by our organization of a wholesale response in this world to what Matthew Arnold called the human instinct for expansion. We do not need to doubt the effectiveness of this wholesale response. We can see it at work in the renaissance of the twelfth century. We see its power to regenerate the human spirit in the sudden widening of its horizons in the sixteenth and seventeenth centuries. It is visible once more in the spaciousness of the American experiment; from the Pilgrim Fathers to the end of the first World War the mere existence of America has been to millions an unceasing source of hope. And it is not less evident that the principles of 1789 have made a similar impact upon the human mind. They have built, as it were, a temple of refuge for the human spirit where there can be preserved that right to dream which, in the last analysis, is the source of man's power to win his mastery over the hostile forces in the universe.

It is, I think, this instinct which the central idea of the Russian Revolution has the capacity to satisfy; and it does not appear that there is any other idea available to us with a similar power. For though the principle of nationalism has evoked passionate response, has been able, even in our own day, to make men die proudly on its behalf, it suffers from the weaknesses, first, that it is on the cultural plane only that it now corresponds to our technological convictions, and, second, that its authority is a compulsion rather to war than to peace at a time when the destructive power of that compulsion is a clear threat to the survival of our civilization. For modern war means not only pestilence and famine; its totalitarian character so lays waste our power to produce that it creates a mass of problems at its close which we are unable either psychologically or economically to solve. It is not, I believe, excessive to argue that the scale of the issues raised by modern war is too massive to be capable of resolution by minds of the calibre of our own. Nothing could, surely, be more significant than the fact that even the United Nations are afraid, as they survey its possible aftermath, to descend from the easy rhetoric of resounding generalization to the difficult realism of concrete action. We can define the large outline of great conceptions like the Four Freedoms. We can express the eager hope that the next age will be the "century of the common man." We can insist that "natural" monopolies must be publicly owned, that the place of consumers' co-operation must be "substantial." But as soon as we move from these peaks of principle to the concrete immediacy of statutes, we prefer to stand in the valley where, in measures like the Catering Act of 1943, we can rest at ease in the fields of traditional action, in the assurance that no large-scale innovation will disturb the unity acceptable to those who have effective power in their hands.

No doubt in the past there have been moments in the history of the great religions when they have obviously possessed the power to elevate the barbarian to that frame of mind where he seeks to discover in service to others the secret of self-respect. But there are good reasons why it is difficult to believe that any of the historic religions has now either the intellectual adequacy or the social relationships which will enable it to satisfy the collective requirements of our civilization, as distinct from its ability to meet the problem of the individual who searches for a reply to the issues of pain and evil. For we must not forget that, until some such period as the Reformation, Christianity, like Judaism, Islam, and Buddhism, sought to make its votaries transcend the problems of human society rather than to solve them. As Rousseau so clearly saw, Christianity was able to build men vowed to the service of God; its weakness was its inability to make men citizens. Its emphasis on a kingdom that was not of this world meant that the issues of social life were an embarrassment to individual salvation, that it cultivated the interior faith of its acolytes, and regarded their external behaviour as less important than their internal faith. The Christian, no doubt, rendered to Cæsar what was Cæsar's own, but he could not, in so far as he was truly Christian, but remember not merely the superior claim of God, but the fact, also, that the definition of this claim was increasingly a matter which the Church claimed to decide as the power of the Empire waned. The Christian was, if not the enemy of the secular world, at least indifferent to it. He was hostile to wealth, hostile to art, hostile to the duty of military defence. And when, after Constantine, he made his terms with the Empire, after that bitter conflict with paganism, of which Salvianus has written so eloquently, he had no message for the poor and the humble for the simple reason that he took no account of poverty or humility since he thought of each as a path to salvation. He was uninterested in the rights of man save as these affected his claim to religious orthodoxy. He did not question the claims of property so long as the doctrine of stewardship was observed. He accepted personal slavery before the Reformation; and he accepted the slavery of the wage system after it.

It is, therefore, an erroneous interpretation of Christianity which sees in it the principles of a revolutionary faith. There were, no doubt, sects within its confines to whom the possession of wealth by Christians, above all by the Christian clergy, seemed a denial of the great end the Church was to serve; but they always failed to do more than make a protest which always failed. And, as the centuries passed, the Church developed the same lust for power as the Empire it had begun by challenging, so that its great officials, a pope or bishop or abbot, were the embodiment of an economic power not less impressive than the parallel secular authority. The supreme test came at the Reformation; Luther's horror at the Peasants' War, and Calvin's acceptance of the new economic order made possible by geographical discovery and scientific development may still have left room for individual consolation; it offered no formula by which the mass of the poor could hope to improve their condition in this world. Nor is there any vital difference, except in chronological adjustment, between the major reformed Churches and that of Rome. By the middle of the sixteenth century, the Jesuits had already entered upon their great task of adapting papal habits to the claims of the new commerce; only the Jansenists expressed an outlook in which the main emphasis remained a medieval one.

All this is not to say for one moment that there were not in every branch of the Christian Churches men who sought to make its creed the basis of a new social order. Peter Waldo, Francis of Assisi, Gerrard Winstanley, James Nayler, in a lesser degree George Fox, had an economic outlook which implied a doctrine far beyond the classic doctrine of the rich man's stewardship of his wealth. But these, and men like these, are by far the exception and not the rule. The Churches, generally speaking, expressed until at least the Industrial Revolution the conviction that what mattered was the conduct of the individual as this bore upon the supreme issue of his salvation; and private grace, rather than collective works, was the criterion by which salvation was decided. After the Industrial Revolution, there is a slow drift towards the development of a Christian social theory, which has a place, greater or less, in all the Christian Churches. But by this time, as notably in France and England, the intellectual case for accepting Christian doctrine has begun rapidly to lose its hold upon the opinion of the masses; and in the Fascist countries even the Christian ethic has been vigorously rejected for the sufficient reason that were it to be practised the status and claims of the Fascist leaders would be incapable of acceptance.

Christian belief, in its orthodox forms, is not so much a code of moral conduct by which men's lives are shaped as a body of conventional principles the enforcement of which enables the society, on the whole, to maintain as much as it can of the traditional relations by putting behind them not merely the coercive power of the state, but, also, the psychological authority which history bestows upon great religious organizations.

This, as I think, emerges with exceptional clarity in the history of the English Church, especially after the Reformation. For it is not only significant that Nonconformity should have been in so large a degree associated with the poorer classes of the community; it is, in some ways, even more significant that the Nonconformist who was economically successful should have gravitated towards the Anglican Church. The Nonconformist Churches of Great Britain provided, since at least the seventeenth century, a body of ideas which were nothing so much as an affirmation of the rights of the poor; and it is this affirmation which built as close a relation between the non-Anglican Protestant Churches and the Labour movement. There was, no doubt, a thread of Christian Socialism throughout the nineteenth century in the Church of England, from F. D. Maurice through Westcott to Bishop Gore and Canon Scott-Holland. Yet it is obvious that the Christian Socialist movement, in its Anglican expression, was a backwater of the Church rather than a part of its central stream. It never was able to reach an expression of strength powerful enough to break, for example, the alliance between the parson and the squire in rural England; and few of the significant figures among the laymen of the Socialist movement had, apart from George Lansbury, the Anglican outlook. It is, indeed, true to say that evangelical Christianity in England was an essential part of the protective rampart of economic *laissez-faire;* and that while Anglicanism, in its Catholic aspect, tended towards a socialist outlook until the time of Charles Gore and Henry Scott-Holland, after the conclusion of the war of 1914–18, the main preoccupation of the Anglo-Catholic movement in Britain was with questions of ritual and liturgy to the exclusion of the social problem.

The Roman Catholic Church has had, of course, its profound manifestations of a socialist tendency. No one can read without emotion, for example, of the great effort of Lamennais in the France of Louis Philippe to put, as one of his critics expressed it, "the red cap on the cross." But, in general, the influence of the Roman Catholic Church has been hostile to either democracy or freedom. Its support of Mussolini in Italy and of Franco in Spain were only the logical outcome of an attitude which, as its suppression of the Spiritual Franciscans made painfully clear, had no difficulty in making its terms with the acquisitive society to which it adapted itself. The principles of 1789 are nothing so much as an attack upon the kind of world for which the authority of Rome has in general stood sponsor ever since the days of Constantine. The Roman Catholic Church may have sponsored trade unions here, and its own peculiar brand of "socialism" there. It may have assisted the struggle for human emancipation when the latter was a necessary, if temporary, concomitant of its own struggle for power. Yet in essential principles, the Roman Catholic Church has taken its colour from those sources in any given environment by alliance with which it could hope for power; it has not sought, save in rare individuals, or in occasional movements, which it has rarely been willing to approve, to communicate the ethos of the Gospels to the societies it has sought to dominate. The history of Rome is not a chapter in the record of human freedom. Rather has it been a means of maintaining any existing complex of interests which was prepared, like Franco in Spain, to find the means of satisfying its claims.[1] Even the semi-liberalism of Leo XIII must be set in the context of the history which precedes and follows it.

Perhaps no documents explain more clearly the conflict between the major Churches and the original faith of the first

---

1 On the remarkable evolution of Spanish Catholicism in recent times there is a brilliant commentary in Gerald Brenan, *The Spanish Labyrinth* (Cambridge, 1943).

Christians than the contrast between the "Declaration of Congregational Societies," [1] issued on November 22, 1647, to vindicate that Church from the accusation of radicalism in social matters, and the remarkable answer to its doctrines which William Walwyn, in some ways the most notable among the left-wing agitators of that age of agitation, called "A Still and Soft Voice." He denounces the superstition of most professing Christians, and notes that they are not merely hostile to the claims of reason, but hateful and persecuting those who are "inquisitive after knowledge." They disdain the poor, save as these share the opinions of the orthodox; and they insist that this disdain enables them the better to serve God and the poor man's soul. "As for his body," wrote Walwyn, "that's no part of his care, he is not so hasty to run into his poore neighbours house, to see what is wanting there, he may ly upon a bed or no bed, covering or no covering, be starved through cold and hunger, over burthened with labour, be sick, lame or diseased . . . he may through want and necessity goe into what prison he will, and ly and rott and starve there: and these kind of Religious people are not halfe so much moved at it, as if he goe to another Church or Congregation then what they approve; and if he doe so, upstarts their zeale; and after him, watch, spy, accuse, and informe; and all for the good of his soule; and for the Glory of God." [2] And Walwyn adds in a striking sentence, "it being not the leaves but the fruit that nourisheth and carrieth the seed with it, shew me thy faith by thy workes; if I have all faith and have not luve, I am as sounding brass, or as a tinckling cymball, if faith workes, it workes by luve." [3]

"If faith workes, it workes by luve"; it is the failure of the major Churches to translate this attitude into a living principle of action which has been responsible for the decline of its influence among the masses. It is, of course, true that Nonconformity has been one of the main sources of the growth of British

[1] Conveniently reprinted in D. M. Wolfe, *Milton in the Puritan Revolution* (New York, 1941), pp. 365–75.

[2] *Ibid.*, p. 369.

[3] *Ibid.*, p. 374.

socialism; but its influence has been indirect rather than direct in character. By emphasizing the claim of the individual to an equal value in the sight of God, it created a demand for recognition of this claim not merely in some life to come but in the world of here and now; and with the growth of industrialization the men who voiced this demand, above all the laymen who voiced it, became, as the nineteenth century proceeded, important architects in the evolution, first of trade-unionism, and then of social legislation which, after the Taff Vale case, required a separate political party for the expression of its purposes. And, with the growth of a separate political Labour Party, the zeal and enthusiasm which, up to some such time as the Dock Strike of 1889, had been in the main expressed in religious organizations, began increasingly to be political rather than religious in expression. The idea of salvation began to receive embodiment in Acts of Parliament which touched, not the life to come, but the earthly activities of men. And, at this point, the hold of the Churches upon their members began in an increasing measure to depend less on the theological dogma they defended than upon the social principles they were prepared to express. It is not, I think, excessive to claim that, between 1918 and 1939, the English Churches were, in the main, concerned, so far as they were influential, with social rather than theological doctrine.

In a formal sense, perhaps, this is less true of the Churches in the United States; though, even there, it is important that the main representatives of American theology have devoted their chief energies to the formulation of a social rather than a theological doctrine. If it cannot be said that this social doctrine points in a particular direction, it is not unfair to claim that the main ethos of the American Churches has been concerned, especially since the war of 1914, less with the life of the next world than with life here and now. No doubt there are Churches, like those of the cotton towns of the South, in which the doctrines taught have been a means of supporting the ideology of the master-class; and there have been prominent figures, like Bishop

Manning of New York, whose social gospel has assumed the validity of the canons of behaviour which the main figures in the politics of "rugged individualism" have sought to impress upon the masses. Fundamentalism, in the narrowest sense of the term, has had its ardent votaries, especially in the South; but it is still true to say that those in the American Churches, Dr. Reinhold Niebuhr, for example, who have given to Christian doctrine a living and progressive content, have sought to make it a body of tenets which fitted the emerging problems of a new world. The American theologian of the inter-war years who sought for influence among the younger generation was driven by the inherent necessity of the claims he confronted, especially after the coming of the great depression, to make his teaching essentially a commentary upon the social issues of the time. What his listeners wanted to know was the relevance of Christianity to the trade unions and to Communism, the work its pastors could do for the unemployed and the intellectually perplexed, rather than to hear them repeat the historical problems connected with the Incarnation or the Atonement.

It is, indeed, reasonable to say that in the United States an interest in the dogmatic problems of the Churches has given place to an interest in their recommendations about behaviour. From this aspect, with the possible exception of the Roman Catholic Church, religious influences for the most part follow, rather than lead, a secular pattern of behaviour the design of which is shaped by the historic development of an acquisitive society which, though its standards be higher than those of the old world, repeats its problems and begets its habits. The American citizen may think of the Churches as the guardian of his moral code and the medium through which he still largely organizes his contributions to charity. But he does not assume that they will shape his way of life. Methodist or Roman Catholic, Unitarian or Congregationalist, he accepts an Americanism which transcends all these. The effective end he desires to reach is a mingling of security and success; and his valuation of religious doctrine is set by the contribution it can make to the achievement of this end. The theology he expects from his religious leaders is, therefore, less dogmatic than pastoral in character. It is help in failure, comfort in trouble, the organization of a service on Sunday which makes him "feel good," or of social entertainment during the week which gives his family the opportunity for a modest pleasure, it is these that he expects his Church and its pastors to provide. It is not a challenge to the worldliness of his daily routine so much as a compensation for its acerbities that he assumes as the function of the Church. The clergyman who is at war with the principles of an acquisitive society is not likely to retain his allegiance for any length of time. For the Church, as he assumes, must "keep out of politics"; and the inference he draws from that obligation is its duty to refrain from any challenge to a secular pattern which has long ceased to find anything in religious dogma which compels the scrutiny, much less the revision, of its foundations. His Church, no doubt, is in the world; but its validity, as a Church, depends upon its acceptance of the world to which it is conditioned. Once it refuses to accept the world, it becomes a threat to the "American way of life"; and an organization which threatens the security of the American way will not be well regarded by the men and institutions to whose support it must look for the means of survival.

The secularization of American religion is not, of course, a late phenomenon; it is obvious at least as early as the publication of Cotton Mather's *Magnalia Christi Americana* in 1702 that the rigorous theology that he represented was already outmoded; the work is an epitaph on past achievements rather than a prophecy of glories to come. And when, in 1717, John Wise wrote his *Vindication of the Government of New England Churches* the way was already half laid which Benjamin Franklin was to complete in the famous chapter on the "Art of Virtue" in his *Autobiography* and in his *Way to Wealth*. The instrumentalism of Franklin may not be quite fairly described, as D. H. Lawrence described it, as an effort to make God an "everlasting Wanamaker," but its main impact was to adapt Christianity, in its traditional form, to the glorification of commercial morality. The Puritan ethos had, of course, already prepared the groundwork for its acceptance. Year by year it prepared the identification of grace with success. The sin of poverty, the duty of effort, the assumption that wealth was a sign of God's favour, the replacement of the feudal hierarchy of power by a hierarchy built on riches, the contempt for idleness, the suspicion of beauty, all of these found their place in the dogmas of Puritan theology. Its result was superbly put by Hawthorne when he wrote that "the entire system of man's affairs, as at present established, is built up purposely to exclude the careless and happy soul. The very children would upbraid the wretched individual who should endeavour to take life and the world as—what we might naturally suppose them meant for—a place and opportunity for enjoyment."

Whether we take the Roman Catholic or the Protestant Churches, the central character of their history is identical. They operate in a world in which the cardinal fact is poverty, and they seek, as best they may, to reconcile the masses to a poverty in which, as Hawthorne saw, the "careless and happy soul" must be excluded. Either they do not examine the exploitation of man by man upon which that poverty is based, or they assume that it is inevitable and seek to secure acceptance of its consequences. Yet either alternative creates for them the difficulty that the Christian ethic, stripped of its unhistorical elements, and, above all, of its eschatological character, is essentially an affirmation of the rights of personality and, thereby, a denunciation of any social order which, by its inequalities, denies that those rights are valid. That is why the Christian who has taken seriously the principles of his faith has always, from the earliest times, been a challenge to the traditional order. He is asking for a world which is incompatible with this world; and that is true whether he be formally Christian like Peter Waldo or Francis of Assisi, or, like Marx or William Morris, is stating its vital principles in terms alien linguistically from the traditional expression. The "Communist Manifesto" and the "Dream of John Ball" have claims to be regarded as, so to say, uncanonical books of scripture which it is not possible to deny unless their rejection is based upon ideas which assume the need for compromise between the philosophy of the Gospels and a social order which rejects the right of personality as such to affirm itself.

The essence of the claim that is made by the idea of the Russian Revolution is almost staggering in its simplicity; and it becomes the more staggering when it is set in its full historical perspective. For it then becomes obvious that the purpose the Revolution is seeking to fulfil is the same purpose as that which, from the dawn, almost, of the record of human effort, has characterized each epoch when a civilization is drawing to its close. The contraction of well-being means the inability to satisfy mass expectation; and there is born, as a rule, out of that inability the slow definition of a faith which seeks to rediscover the conditions upon which the satisfaction may be renewed. The effort at definition begets, in its turn, at once a movement which seeks to give substance to that faith, and a fear, in those whose well-being depends upon the maintenance of the ancient ways, that the movement may threaten their safety. All this is clear in the history of the Russian Revolution; almost a century elapsed between the first protest of the Decembrists and the final expression of their effort in the victory of Lenin and the Bolsheviks. And when one analyses the character of these hundred years, stripped of the elements peculiar to Russian conditions, the principles that seem to emerge are the same as those which underlie the dream of the early Christians, the English civil wars of the seventeenth century, 1789, and 1848. There is a sense, hardly less vital, in which the war of 1914 is the first act in a drama in which there is emerging once more an idea of an essentially similar kind. Of course there is ebb and flow in the development of the idea, as in each of the previous expressions of its power. That is clear in the English Revolution of the seventeenth century; what triumphed there was, no doubt, a victory for human freedom, but it was not a victory, as the Clarke Papers make so manifest, in the results of which the masses had a serious share. That was clear, again, in the Revolution of 1789; there was a profound liberation in the victory of the Third Estate; but the defeat of 1940 offered a striking proof that the rich *bourgeoisie* which was carried to power by the *sans-culottes* did not recognize in the latter any claim to share in that fulfilment which depends upon the legal relations of property. And, in the same way, in the February Revolution of 1917, the men who overthrew the Tsar were not thinking that a new Russia might be organized in which the common man had a status independent of his property rights; it was not until the return of Lenin from his exile that the masses were made to understand the kind of world it was in their power to shape.

And, from the moment when the October Revolution was consummated, the forces of privilege began to organize the overthrow of its results. Not in Russia alone, but all over the world reaction planned the counter-revolution. Its votaries denied each expression of power, political or economic or social, which jeopardized their special claims. When Mussolini overthrew democracy in Italy, the world resounded to their applause. When Hitler established his gangster autocracy in Germany, they were still prepared to recognize in his system a method of governance as valid as any other. When the Spanish people threw off the yoke of centuries, they invented the doctrine of non-intervention that evil and ruthless privilege might recover its ancient rights. Poland, Rumania, Yugoslavia, Greece, in each of these the counter-revolution was completed with hardly a word of protest from democratic statesmen. We know, of course, that their judgment is naturally related to the situation they occupy. No Englishman is likely, at least since 1940, to forget the debt this country owes to Mr. Churchill, but no historian, either, in assessing Mr. Churchill's judgment of the inter-war years is likely to forget, when the full account is cast, that, in 1927, when he was Chancellor of the Exchequer, Mr. Churchill spoke with enthusiasm of Mussolini's "gentle and simple bearing," and of his "detached poise in spite of so many burdens and dangers." "If I had been an Italian," Mr. Churchill said, "I am sure that I should have been with you wholeheartedly from start to finish in your triumphant struggle against the bestial appetites and passions of Leninism." [1] Mr. Churchill, of course, is a specialist in rhetoric, and, not least, in those adjectival decorations which give to rhetoric its power of popular appeal. The Mussolini of 1927 was already the self-confessed murderer of Matteoti and Amendola, and he had slain in Italy most of the dreams out of which the common man marches to his emancipation. His prisons were full; his censorship was complete; and his special police already had their grim watch over every family which did not conform to his wishes. So that Mr. Churchill was eulogizing a Mussolini in whom no element of today was absent save his willingness to assist Hitler in effecting the destruction of Great Britain. What, in the years after 1927, Mr. Churchill resented in Mussolini was not his embodiment of the counter-revolutionary principle, but the direction of his energy against the interests of Great Britain. When it was directed against Spain or Albania, Mr. Churchill remained unmoved.

Yet over against this counter-revolution which is, above all, the effort of the few to maintain their privileges against the claims of the many, there stand certain general lessons to the value of which all history since the civilization of Greece and Rome bears witness. Above all, the truth is self-evident that we are members one of another. My neighbour's well-being is directly related to my own; if I injure him, I am bound, in the nature of things, to injure myself. Nor can it be doubted that a civilization based on what Carlyle called the "cash-nexus" has no ultimate chance of survival. It enables men to build a relationship with one another; but the evidence is almost unbearably clear that this relationship will never grow into the kind of fellowship where men feel a genuine responsibility for the well-being of one another. And it is grimly clear that where that temper of fellowship is absent, there is bound to be, whether between nations or classes, that sense of exploitation of which the

---

1 Speech of January 20, 1927. I owe this illuminating quotation to the *Tribune* of July 30, 1943.

ultimate result is war. The Peasants' Revolt in England in 1381, the Peasants' War in Germany in the sixteenth century, the wars of religion in France, the Civil War in the United States, are all of them classic examples of what happens in a commonwealth when the privilege of the few is bought at the expense of the suffering of the many. And conflict within is matched by conflict without. Spain and France and Germany seek to dominate the Western world that they may escape the horror of internal war; they are willing to use the exclusive passion which nationalism breeds in the hope, always in the end a vain hope, that they may escape the hatred bred within by the sense of injustice felt by the many when they are compelled to be slaves to the few.

Nor is this all. There is a grim truth in Paine's famous aphorism that government is due to our wickedness. The law does not mean the rule of justice; it means, as de Maistre said, that the executioner is the corner-stone of society. We appoint judges and fill prisons and inflict punishments which defame the quality that human nature might possess because our laws of property in an acquisitive society make our neighbours our enemies and not our friends. They make the atmosphere in which we act not one of mutual aid but one of general exploitation. We employ—no word could be more telling—not men but "hands"; we replace men by women for the sake of cheapness. We think not of the amenities we could enjoy in common by separating the idea of work from the payment of wages, but of the wealth we can individually accumulate upon which will be built the power and esteem we exercise. We seek, in such a society, to maintain the ultimate contradiction which bids us worship God and Mammon at one and the same time. But the worship of God, where it is real, is a frustration of our worship of Mammon; and it becomes something like a revolutionary protest which the worship of Mammon, if in its turn it is real, is bound to define as a seditious act and against which it must bring to bear the whole apparatus of coercive power of which the state disposes. Because the two purposes are incompatible with one another in their ideal form, either one becomes the servant of the other, and establishes an orthodoxy in the name of which it moves at once to intolerance and persecution, or they mean that our lives are frustrated by our inability to build our philosophy of action upon common assumptions in which all citizens share. Where the conflict is real, as in our own age, the commonwealth has no genuine semblance of unity. Its classes lead different lives; their members speak a different language; and the common stock of welfare that we might relate to common needs is divided without relation either to effort or to service. A society of this kind is in reality no more than a vast hospital in which what there remains in our leaders of a sense of shame compels them to keep alive men and women whose death our conscience does not permit us to secure. And we try to lull our conscience into somnolence by emphasis upon the Pharisaic dogma that poverty is an inevitable condition which, even if it were removed, would return by the operation of the laws of nature because amongst us there are stupid men, lazy and inefficient. The acquisitive society, we protest, is nothing less than the outcome of the scriptural warning that we shall always have the poor in our midst. So that poverty, with its ill health and mean houses, and ugly ignorance, is simply the outcome of a world in which the inequality which the law promotes is a reflection of the natural order in which we tell ourselves we are inescapably involved.

And, given a society based, as ours is based, upon the acquisitive principle, there is little hope that it can fulfil, in any profound way, the ideal of fraternity. For as soon as it attaches importance to its citizens upon the basis not of the service they can render one another, but of the property they can acquire, it is inevitable that it will attach importance not to their identities, but to their differences; and the whole mechanism of its legal institutions will be devoted not to the achievement of an equal response to equal needs but to the maintenance of the different response its system of ownership compels to needs that are, in fact, perceived to be equal whenever the society is threatened by a common danger. There is a sense, indeed, in which nothing is more fantastic in our society than the way in which, during each of the two world wars, the promise of fraternity as the basis of our social life has become part of the professional rhetoric of political perorations, and the way in which, also, as the democracies overcome the danger they relapse out of the enthusiasm for fraternity into that relationship of class war which is the normal condition between citizens who have the security that property gives and citizens who have nothing but their labour-power to sell. I suspect, indeed, that it is not accident that both the teaching of Jesus and the doctrine of the "Communist Manifesto" are at one in their emphasis upon the danger of the family, which, in an acquisitive society, acts as a barrier between men and women instead of a link which binds them together. For it is the central faith, alike of the Gospels and of socialism, that there is neither Jew nor Greek, neither bond nor free; but where the claim of son upon parents, or brother upon brother, is set in terms of the view that proximity of relationship means that one's property is proportionately available to one's kin also, the family becomes the nurse of avarice and narrowness, a hindrance, rather than a help, to fraternity in the commonwealth.

If it be said that this outlook is an impractical one, that it denies the human nature that we know, there are, I conceive, two final answers. The first is that we move at once towards the plane we call impractical the moment that we feel our society is threatened. The history of all epochs when social existence is in danger is the record of our ability to work a system which evokes willingly from most a level of morale far higher than the one with which we rest content in times of ease. And the theory that this outlook is a contradiction of human nature is, very obviously, a confusion between man's nature and the behaviour to which he is conditioned by the system under which he dwells. It is beyond dispute that if a threat to the existence of the society brings out of men qualities of energy and devotion and self-sacrifice which they do not display in the absence of that threat, they have within them the impulses which makes the higher level of conduct possible; and the descent from that level is then not something compelled by their nature, but evoked as a conditioned response by the environment in which they live. So, to take an obvious example, the social conditions of the Greek city-state made slavery appear a "natural" thing to Aristotle; but it is certain that neither a political philosopher nor a party leader today would venture to make the restoration of slavery a part of his doctrine or his programme on the ground that a rational analysis of human nature proved it to be "natural."

Most of us have little difficulty in seeing that this is the case with a condition like personal slavery which has ceased to be the basis of our economic life. We ought to remember that what applies to our view of slavery, applies, with equal force, to many other conditions deemed "natural" only a brief period since our own day. It is, after all, only a century since Macaulay's speech on the Ten Hours Law limited by state regulation the length of the working day. It is barely three-quarters of a century since compulsory elementary education was made part of the general social outlook of a British citizen. It is barely a generation since national insurance against sickness and unemployment was made a normal element in the habits of our people. In each of these cases—and they are chosen from a mass of analogous instances—the behaviour implied in the rule enforced by the state-power has become so "natural" that we find it difficult to realize that there are people still alive to whom these changes represented an innovation almost revolutionary in its proportions. We are driven, I think, from the experience of this rapidly changing world to accept the assumption upon which de Tocqueville rightly placed so much emphasis, that what we call "necessary" institutions are no more than institutions to which over a period we have become habituated, and that in the field of social matters the possibilities of innovation are far wider and more profound than we are normally accustomed to imagine.

And if this be granted, it is, I think, legitimate to infer that the *Realpolitik* of an acquisitive society may well derive from a view of human nature which fails to evoke the full potentialities of dignity and devotion of which it is capable. If we assume that the power to acquire is the test of a man's place among his fellows, it then becomes "natural" to assume that the greatest man is he who can acquire the most. And if we add to that assumption the further inference that the power to acquire will measure, in a general way, the political authority of him who acquires, we shall be led quite simply to believe, like President Coolidge, that, since Mr. Andrew W. Mellon is among the half-dozen outstanding millionaires in the United States, he may naturally be regarded as "the greatest Secretary of the Treasury since Hamilton." Or if we begin by assuming that the doctrines of which Lenin was the exponent indicate "bestial appetites and passions," then, like Mr. Churchill in 1927, we shall be driven by the inherent logic of that postulate to shower upon Mussolini the eulogies which, in the changed situation since 1940, Mr. Churchill has, no doubt, been eager to forget. The part of wisdom is, pretty clearly, to be prudent enough to recognize that the malleability of human nature is far greater than statesmen, with a special axe to grind at a special time, are willing to admit. And once this range of potential behaviour is granted, the acquisitive society becomes merely one of the forms of social behaviour through which the impulses of man receive expression. The possibility then, lies open that it is not the only form, and that we can experiment with confidence upon the assumption that there are alternatives which exclude the idea of acquisition as the vital motive to which all human conduct must be conditioned.

There have been, of course, in the past, moments in the history of the great religions when they have obviously possessed the power to elevate ordinary men to that frame of mind where they are eager to discover the secret of self-respect. But it is difficult to believe either that these moments will recur, or that any of the great religions has now either the social content or the intellectual adequacy which enables it to satisfy the requirements of a civilization as distinct from its ability to meet the problem of the individual who searches for a reply to the issues of pain and evil. That the religious mystic will always find in some personal faith the sources of a private consolation I do not for a moment deny. Obviously enough, that inner light which shone in men like Saint John of the Cross or George Fox, which captured the hearts of worldly men like Ignatius Loyola or William Penn, will shine in them whatever be the habits of our civilization. The ultimate mystery of the universe will never be revealed to us; and those who can penetrate behind the veil which hides its secret will always be a chosen few whose vision is more likely to be private to themselves than a common insight in which the masses can share. For the outlook which is preserved, for example, in those noble last words of James Nayler requires a temperament of genius which separated its possessor from the normal level of mankind.[1] Not only is it alien from the environment to which most of us belong; it is also destroyed, for most, by the critical examination of the testimony upon which it depends. Some three hundred years of historical scholarship have been fatal to the claims of any revealed religion which offers the promise of personal salvation to its adherents. The life of each of us is outside any sphere in which we are entitled to permit the escape of categories of experience from a reality which would be capable, if we had the knowledge, of explanation in scientific terms.

I am not for one moment denying the validity of religious revelation for those rare and special persons who find in an experience private to themselves a reality which transcends the reality in which ordinary men and women share. When Isaac Penington writes [2] that "this is He whom I have waited for and sought after from my childhood" it is folly to deny that it is upon the reality so discovered that all his life will be based so long as the power of that emotion continues into which he so enters. In that sense, no doubt, religion is as old as civilization

[1] James Nayler, *Works* (1716), p. 696.
[2] Isaac Penington, *Works* (ed. of 1761), I, xxxvii–xxxviii.

and will last as long as human beings possess, however rarely, the gift which brings with it the conviction that they have pierced the veil in which, for most of us, the problems of the universe are shrouded. I am arguing the very different thesis that a religious experience based on the claim that it is valid when tested by the canons of scientific evidence, and, because so tested, is entitled to assume the form of an ecclesiastical organization which may exact the allegiance of mankind, that such experience has no longer any validity for our age. To the degree that we look to such experience as the means of elevating collective well-being, we are giving our confidence to a method which is bound, sooner or later, to fail.

This is not to say that ecclesiastical organizations have not had their epochs of great achievement; I think they have had them and that, in those periods, they have brought new hope to the communities they have influenced by the faith they have been able to impose. But the hope so brought is not a permanent thing; sooner or later it becomes adapted to the general character of the social environment in which it operates. This is surely true of the Church of Rome after its adoption by the Empire; it is true of the Reformation Churches; it is true even of that Society of Friends, which, of all the Christian sects, has remained most faithful to the ideal of its founders. There comes a stage in the development of all of them when they seek to make their peace with the world they had come to transform; and they accept the price of that peace, which is the acquisition of wealth and power. So that an organization which sets out to enable its members to achieve salvation by the transcendence of reality ends by conforming to that reality it was its purpose to transcend. That is why, for example, in the literature of the Reformation the Rome which was to its votaries the owner of the keys of heaven had become, alike for Lutheran and Calvinist, the embodiment of antichrist. Professor Lynd has noted, in his second study of Middletown, the decline in religious feeling; his working man who remarked, "I don't go to church because the church ought to have something to meet the needs of labouring men, and the labourers feel that the administration of churches is in the hands of wealth," is only saying more simply what he reports a physician who is in close touch with the life of the city was saying, that "the average citizen has very definite religious beliefs, but for the most part they are a kind of automatic part of the scheme of inherited things, and not anything he uses particularly in his daily life." [1] That is perhaps why when the minister of the largest local church preached, in 1936, upon the reasons why he intended to vote for Roosevelt, he himself expected to lose his post, and the result was a mixture of comment which varied from the expression of doubt about his mental condition to the affirmation of a local journal that political commentary is out of place in the pulpit.[2] It is assumed, in short, in Middletown, as elsewhere, that it is not the business of the Churches to define the system of values by which men's lives are shaped.

Now if the Churches are thus content to abandon that role of leadership which enabled Christianity, in its first challenge to Western civilization, to be accepted as the basis upon which the religious values and convictions of men were built, it is clear that the source of leadership must be looked for elsewhere. For in an epoch in which, as in our own, the central values of society are in the melting pot, men look for guidance to the men or to the organization which has the power and the faith to redefine those values. If the Churches lack that power and that faith, there are two alternatives. One is the prospect that it is everywhere lacking, so that the civilization, lacking any executive guidance, moves, even if slowly, still with relentless certainty, to catastrophe; the other is the prospect that the leadership which the Churches abandon may be found elsewhere. What is, I suggest, quite certain is that in our present phase of development there is no section of the intellectuals in whom the chance of a revitalized faith can be recognized. For whether we take the poets or the novelists, the dramatists or the critics,

---

1 Robert S. and Helen M. Lynd, *Middletown in Transition* (1937), p. 302.

2 *Ibid.*, p. 310.

the main feature of their outlook is its negativism. And that feature comes from nothing so much as the anxiety to achieve perfection of form, and to avoid content lest this be regarded, as in the Churches, as taking sides in a conflict where the artist's duty is to remain above the battle. It is even argued, as by M. Benda, that the intellectuals, by their refusal to teach "other religions than the religion of the material," have failed in their mission and been guilty of a betrayal of exactly that civilization it was their obligation to save.

It would be easy to show that the intellectuals, Sorel, Kipling, Maurras, Barrès, Péguy, whom M. Benda has singled out for condemnation are, in fact, but a small platoon in the great army corps that any serious discussion of the subject would call for; and it would be still easier to prove that the men of letters whom he attacks are, in fact, the reflection of our social conditions, rather than their cause. For it is now too obvious to need elaborate documentary proof that those who attributed the French Revolution to the *philosophes* of the eighteenth century omitted to explain why the *philosophes* were able to attain so vast an influence in so brief a space of time; and what is true of the *philosophes* is still more true of the explanation which finds the causes of the Revolution hidden in a secret conspiracy of *Illuminati* and Freemasons. The appeal of Voltaire and Rousseau in the eighteenth century in France was, no doubt, in part due to the sheer quality of their power of expression; but it was due also, in a degree that it is difficult to make of less importance, to the fact that they said what the iniquity and corruption of the *ancien régime* predisposed men to hear. The literature of an age is inevitably an expression of the problems of that age, and of the ability of the men to find, even to want to find, a solution to them. Anyone who looks at the work of the Encyclopædists can see, as with the great Victorians, that all their creative energy is directed not to matters of pure form but to issues which they wish to define in their way rather than in another way. They are not detached from those issues, and they do not seek to be above the battle that is being waged. Rather, like

Heine, they see it as part of their task to be soldiers in that battle.

The tragedy of the intellectuals of our time has been their relative indifference to one of the supreme battles in the history of civilization, or, alternatively, that, like Sorel and Kipling, like Barrès and Maurras, and, if in a lesser degree, even Charles Péguy, they had enlisted in the army of reaction. It is worth noting that there is hardly an evil against which Dickens and Charles Reade, Ruskin and Matthew Arnold and William Morris warned the Victorians which has not, as it has been neglected, poisoned our social organization. The crime of the intellectuals was not, as Benda thought, that some of them went into the battle. The crime was the very different one that most of them did not know that a battle was being waged, and that, of those who did, a majority was willing to fight on the wrong side. It was not merely that, as in the war of 1914, the men of letters and the artists were willing, with rare exceptions, to glorify the conflict and even take pride in the effectiveness with which they served a social order the decadence of which was proved by the fact of war. What was even worse was the fact that, when the peace came in 1919, they entered the waste land instead of embarking upon the task of reconstruction. Occasionally, we listened to the voice of a poet who, like W. H. Davies, had the great gift of natural song. Occasionally, also, some angry sonnet of Mr. Siegfried Sassoon would show that the poet's divine power of passionate anger could still express itself. But that Mr. T. S. Eliot should have been the outstanding influence in Anglo-American poetry between the two wars is not less significant than Professor Lynd's report of a Christianity which, as in Middletown, has come to terms with the money-changers in return for the right to retain a small room in the temple.

It was not that Mr. Eliot had not great gifts, learning, the power of superb phrase, a mastery of the ironic epithet unsurpassed in our time. But the most important thing in Mr. Eliot was his horror of the common man, his shrinking from any contact with the masses, the fastidious sensitiveness which seemed to regard whatever is democratic as in its nature vulgar and ugly and barbarous. Mr. Eliot showed, as no other poet of his time, that we were reaching the end of a culture as surely as in the days when Claudian celebrated in his epic the last great triumph of Roman poetry. For he neither sought nor desired to make his music heard by ordinary people. He spoke to an *élite* the real pride of which lay in its deliberate cultivation of remoteness from ordinary people. There was no spontaneity of feeling in what he wrote, but rather a mannered disdain for a world in which the overwhelming majority would have no more chance of understanding his poems than they would of following a paper by Einstein or some development by Littlewood of the mathematical theory of inequalities. If it be said that it is not the business of an eminent poet to write so that the half-literate masses may follow his thought, it is surely a sufficient answer that the cultivation of a conscious aloofness from the world is at least as artificial a procedure as a refusal to write down to the level of the masses. When the poet ceases to be Shelley's "unacknowledged legislator of the world," it is because he has ceased to find meaning in the world; he has so divorced thought from action that he has hardly wanted even an audience to address. The poet who thus cuts himself off from his fellows is cutting himself off from life. And that is, as hardly anything else can be, a denial that life has meaning. For the poet to whom his art denies the necessity of the fullest communication that is open to him is in truth denying that he has anything it is essential to say. His art becomes a form of narcissism in which he whispers to himself, afraid, above all, lest he be overheard; and even when, as with Mr. Eliot, he writes with brilliance for a special band of acolytes, it is rather the echo of his own voice than the message he has to proclaim that is of importance to him. At that point, surely, what has withered in him is humanism, and he has exchanged the full range of imaginative insight for a mysticism which blacks out the living world. I cannot think that it is the function of poetry thus to deny the validity of life. But the poet who performs this function is as profoundly guilty as any of those whom M. Benda impeaches of the treason of which he accuses them. Like the Desert Fathers, he has gone into self-chosen exile because he fears the battle which is waging. That is an abandonment of the positive life which it is difficult to distinguish from betrayal of it.

I am not arguing that one ought to criticize Mr. Eliot because the view he recommends to us has become, in fact, a tradition based on values which repose on both sanctions and on hopes which are largely irrelevant not only to our problems but, also, to the dearly purchased achievements of modern historical scholarship. Every society in crisis produces small groups of thinkers who seek to provide, as Mr. Eliot has sought, an alternative outlook to the predominant habits of thought in and through which he finds release from the misery these cause him. No one can read Mr. Eliot's writings without the admiring conviction that he loathes with all his heart the degradation it imposes by the standards to which it is committed. No one, either, can doubt his deep anxiety to find a way out of that degradation.

My criticism is the different one, first, that he accepts as inevitable that degradation for all but a small band of precious souls, and, second, that this leads him to address these only in what is almost wilfully a special language in the obscurities of which he quite obviously has a peculiar pleasure; he thus deliberately turns his back upon the supreme issue of whether it is in our power to elevate the standards of value and taste throughout our society; one is always reminded, in reading Mr. Eliot, of the great Hebrew scholar, Dr. Schechter's remark, of Oxford —"they mistake fastidiousness for holiness." I accept the fact not only that he has given profound satisfaction to his disciples, even that he has expressed the disillusion of this generation more vividly than any other contemporary figure. But I suspect that the satisfaction he has given them derives less from the inherent beauty of what he has written than from the fact that, as they apprehend the meaning of his exotic remoteness, they are made to feel that they, too, by that power to apprehend, are set apart, with their master, from the multitude.

So that the real effect of Mr. Eliot's work is to abandon the great mass of men and women to those who impose upon our civilization the very standards he is denouncing. He has, so to say, found his way out of the waste land through a door he leaves half-hidden still, even while he proclaims that no one can find the clue to salvation unless he passes through that door. So that those who through poverty, or the ills, physical and social and cultural, which accompany it, not merely receive no call to seek for the vision he himself has seen; Mr. Eliot seems to have a sense almost of delight in insisting that a glimpse of the vision is beyond their powers. The character our society gives to men leads him to an almost Platonic disdain of ordinary persons, and the inference that they are unfit to join the pilgrimage on which he has set out; and, alongside that inference, he turns round to denounce them fiercely for their refusal to see the beauty and the truth of the vision he is painting. He leaves them to struggle in a corruption they did not cause, and blames them contemptuously for not perceiving the depth of their corruption. The note of disdain and contempt for the masses is omnipresent; and I call this a betrayal of culture, a form of intellectual treason, because it leaves those prisoners of the dark forces in society to whom it might have sought to communicate their way to emancipation. It is important, moreover, to add with emphasis that, in terms of the Christian tradition to which Mr. Eliot seeks a return, the contrast between the massive simplicity of its founders, with their deliberate appeal to the poor and the humble and the despised, and the complex aloofness of its restatement, is significant indeed. It is the measure in which the democratic ideal is assumed to be unmeaning and impossible. Values are confined to an aristocracy which stands apart and remote from the daily struggle.

I agree at once that it is not the task of imaginative literature to be didactic; still more, that the inculcation of any specific creed is not a duty to which any of the arts is called. I agree that the artist must report what he sees, and that, if he dons the uniform of a Church or a party, there is danger that his vision will be dimmed. But great literature cannot be either a means of escape merely from the tragic burden of life, nor can it seek to provide the artist with no more than a means of self-realization without regard to the price society pays for that fulfilment. For the logic of that view becomes, in the end, the claim that the rest of mankind must be content to be no more than instruments who make possible the artist's godlike satisfaction. Great art, in all its media, is surely the communication of an intense emotion which, at its deepest level, gives new insight to all who hear its call. It seeks to be an understanding shared, not a secret withheld. Whether it is Homer singing his epic into the memory of all Greek history, or Paul of Tarsus journeying in endless anxiety to communicate his good tidings, the function it performs is a spiritual elevation which reaches the higher the more supreme its quality. In the degree that it withdraws its secret, and leaves the masses in the waste land, it leaves them, also, to become the victims of men like Hitler and Mussolini, of mean cults and ugly illusions, of the crude habits which mistake power and pomp for truth and beauty. And, in the end, the artist shares the fate of the masses he thus abandons; for when they have lost their power to differentiate between good and evil, between great art and poor art, they enter a prison whose jailer demands from the artist himself that he announce no message which might make his captives seek to break their prison bars. Great artists can only be free when they call the world to freedom.

What I have said of the poet like Mr. Eliot, seems to me true, in an even greater degree, of the intellectualist like James Joyce in the realm of fiction. *Ulysses* and its successor, *Finnegans Wake,* are capable, no doubt, of various interpretations; and it is obvious that no novel published between the two world wars even approaches it in technical accomplishment or in the influence it has exerted on the younger generation. But what is, I think, important in Joyce's work, from the angle of its social significance, is the proof that it offers in the case of the novel, as Mr. Eliot offers proof in the case of poetry, that the values of the society it represents are in a state of final and decisive decay. It is not merely, to take *Ulysses* only, that the day in the life of

Leopold Bloom is a mass of obscene frustration; what is still more important is the fact that by making the stream of consciousness in Bloom a complete universe in which the objective facts of existence and their relations have no reality save as ideas which Bloom experiences, Joyce pushes the individualism of contemporary culture to a point where it is drained of all social meaning. It is built upon an inescapable logic which assumes the finality of subjectivism. But in fulfilling the end to which this logic leads it makes madness the king of the mind, so much the king that the ordinary language of communication no longer is adequate to convey the meaning the artist is anxious to report. And the thesis which underlies the whole construction is, despite its marvellous technique, the insistence that events occur without order or relation, that they are devoid of quality, that, in its final phase, the mind of the individual, when taken as an ultimate, has no prospect of attaining values because it is incapable of achieving relations. It has reduced the whole universe to a mood in its subconscious, and, in the very process of that reduction, it has destroyed the universe. There is a sense in which Joyce made more evident than any writer of his time the decisive bankruptcy of the civilization he had so carefully studied with so consummate a mastery.

Joyce, it may be said, was after all deliberately concerned to escape from reality; despite the vital importance of the influence he exercised, it is not fair to choose him as an example of the intellectual. But it is at least fair to note that the supreme artist in the field of fiction in the inter-war years could only, as it were, meet the issues of life by refusing to face them at all. And if we exclude Joyce as exceptional, despite the immensity of his impact, and turn to a novelist who poses with engaging frankness and ability all the issues of our age, to Mr. Aldous Huxley, it is difficult to feel, despite his learning and his skill and the measured scrupulosity with which each problem is posed, that the bankruptcy is, at bottom, any less startling than that of Mr. Joyce. He is certain that the society which exists is utterly barren. He emphasizes the abyss which separates it from the artist.

He sees a decisive divergence between the outlook of those who toil and of those who create. He sees little or no richness of spirit in the world about us, and what culture it has built is pretty vigorously condemned. Mr. Huxley, with engaging candour, presents us with a world in which the comfortable middle class and the intellectual have so completely lost their way that the only outcome of contemplating their lives is a mixture of despair and of disgust. Mr. Huxley is, perhaps, especially interesting because beneath this mixture there is so clearly an ardent Puritan whose main quality is the depth of his conviction of man's original sin.

And it cannot, I think, be said that Mr. Huxley's positive remedies for our condition take us very far on the road to liberation. A conviction that war is wholly evil, an insistence that we dare not divorce the means we use from the ends we seek, an ardent eulogy of Mr. F. Mathias Alexander's theories of posture, and a suggestion that we become free men in the degree that, like Père Joseph, we conquer that inner self which is compounded of lusts of the flesh and the desire for power—these seem to be the sources to which Mr. Huxley looks for our salvation. It is difficult not to feel that, even taken together, they are rather an evasion of his problem than a remedy for it. To preach the pacifist doctrine in the era of the greatest war the world has ever known is, objectively, at least, to range oneself on Hitler's side. To insist that means and ends are inseparable is not very helpful until we make the attempt Mr. Huxley has consistently avoided, the definition of ends and the consequential choice of means proportionate to their achievement. Enthusiasm for Mr. Alexander's theories of posture is a luxury that one admits as a right in Mr. Huxley as one admits the right of Mr. Shaw to champion, since he so desires it, the cause of anti-vivisection. But it is less easy to admit the theory upon which the portrait of Père Joseph has been so skilfully painted. For when all allowance is made for the diplomat's passion for flagellation and his immersion in a mysticism into which his political activities were not permitted to enter, the Père Joseph who matters in history is the co-operator in the power politics of Cardinal Richelieu; and it is difficult not to conclude that both the flagellation and the mysticism were no more than a penance imposed upon him by his better self for activities as a diplomatic emissary of which he was, with good reason, ashamed. The fact therefore remains that Mr. Huxley has never seriously confronted, in novel or in essay, the burning issues which are destroying the very foundations of our social system. His conclusion appears to be that most of the men and women it breeds are not worth saving, but that a few chosen souls may reach that state of grace where the wide vision and the deep insight enable the artist to transcend the meanness of a grim reality from which the masses have no hope of escape.

As one reads, in fact, the literature of Western Europe and the United States in the inter-war years, it is difficult not to be reminded, behind all the superficial differences of attitude and expression, of the medieval conception of an hierarchical society in which the power of birth is replaced by the power of wealth. There is in the ruling class the same mixture of disdain and sympathy, not unmixed with fear. The poverty and insecurity of the great depression can be paralleled by the passionate complaints of the fifteenth century. If there is a brave Archbishop in our own day, there are eminent ecclesiastics, like Nicolas de Clémanges or the great Gerson, who speak boldly in favour of reform. The politicians who speak at the States-General present the complaints of the poor much as a member of Parliament for a constituency in the distressed areas spoke on behalf of his electorate. The suffering of the poor is a favourite motif in the chronicler and the poet; Jean Meschinot asks of God that He will look on, and provide speedily for, the indigence of the common people. There is even, as in the famous sermon of John Ball during the revolt of 1381, the emphasis upon the idea of the equality of men.[1]

But, in our period, as in the earlier time, the sense of pity is

---

1 On this see J. Huizinga, *The Waning of the Middle Ages* (1937), *passim,* and especially Chapter III.

a stereotyped commonplace which does not lead to the demand for action, and is ready to insist that pity is dangerous the moment it expresses itself in agitation. Pity has no programme because it is always an inadequate substitute for justice. It ignores relations and institutions in order to devote itself to the claims of persons. And here, once more, what emerges is the emphasis upon the individual, the antithesis between the acquisitive impulse and the social purpose which prevents that unity upon which a true commonwealth depends. The Victorian poet and novelist may have had self-confidence; but its basis is not merely their belief that it is their duty to attack the evils they see, it is also their assurance that the evil has its remedy. The poet and the novelist of our time both lack that sense of inner confidence, and they are mostly afraid to attack the evils of their age lest they stir up those dangerous scourges which let loose upon a society a revolution of which they cannot predict the outcome. So that their pity, like that of their predecessors in the fifteenth century, arises not from a judgment pronounced but from a cry overheard. And even their pity is mostly expressed in a special language and a peculiar tone suitable to a cultivated class which has found escape from the bitterness of reality and dare not seek to face it again. For while they loathe, like Mr. Eliot, the waste land in which they dwell, have even a deep conviction of impending change, they fear even more the unknown future that this change may bring. So that they do not dare, in any decisively creative way, to give a lead to their generation. What they ask is rather that our rulers shall somehow manage to make enough concessions to maintain the compromise which renders it possible to avoid breakdown. They suspect that the old order is dead; but they cannot bring themselves with a stout heart to give their help to the birth of the new.

The disintegration of our time, with all its ugly consequences, is sometimes seen from a different angle. Western culture is the product of a system of complex relationships to which Hellenism and Hebraism have both made their contributions; but its inner and ultimate unity, we are told, lies in the synthesis of these by the Christian Church, which disciplined Europe to its implications, and enabled its peoples to share in, and be shaped by, the training they received in this massive school. The sanctions of the civilized habits it made possible are, we are told, to be found in the fact that Rome has sought consistently to make the great idea of natural law the criterion of all political behaviour so that at the base of our common life is Christendom, with ideas which reach beyond all national boundaries, with a mission which alone has the Divine Spirit to refresh and guide its members to the healing of our disintegration, and thence, to the recovery of our unity. It is as we have lost the will to be Christian that we have lost the power to make our fellows see that no values count save those which are eternal. Only as we find that will once more shall we regain the right to hope.

This outlook is expressed in a variety of forms, for an agreement upon what is Christianity is not easily come by in a world where Churches and sects are not merely almost beyond count, but still willing enough each to doubt that the others possess the true way to salvation. The eminent Roman Catholic historian, Mr. Christopher Dawson, for example, believes that this disintegration began with the Reformation, and there is an important sense in which, behind the kindly rampart of his learning, one can see that he views [1] the confusion and evil of our times not very differently from the way in which it was viewed by Bossuet and de Maistre. The famous phrase of de Maistre, indeed, "*point de pape, point d'église; point d'église, point de réligion*" almost tumbles into the margins of Mr. Dawson's pages, though he is far too skilful and subtle a controversialist to allow it full right of entrance. But his chain of argument leads to the same conclusion. Multiplicity of Churches made for secularization; secularization made reason of state a threat to natural law; one shall only evade the danger of that threat by rebuilding our unity in religious truth; and Mr. Dawson argues that no one can read the great Encyclicals which have come from the Vatican since the time of Leo XIII without seeing that it is by a return to the

[1] *The Judgment of the Nation* (London, 1943).

acceptance of the leadership of Rome that we may alone hope to exorcise the demons by whom we are beset on every side.

The problem is not only far less simple than Mr. Dawson makes it; more, it is matter for dismay that it should present itself to him in this form. For, first of all, the Reformation was not the work of evil men; an outsider may be permitted to remark that no serious student can study the lives of Luther and Zwingli and Calvin without the conviction that, whatever their defects, whether of conduct or of habit of mind, they were not less passionate in their desire to establish the Kingdom of God upon earth than any of their papal opponents. And, if it be said that one of the evil results of the Lutheran dispensation was to confer an excessive authority on all secular power, so that there is a quite real sense in which it is true to say that his victory laid one, at least, of the main pillars of Prussianism, there is the not less significant fact that the Spanish monarchy has been, for centuries, the spoiled partner of the Vatican, and that Franco is as much the expression of its purposes as was Frederick the Great the outcome of Luther's victory.[1] The character of the Roman Catholic Church in the era of Luther is one of the fundamental causes of that victory. If we could restore the unity which then was—I think irreparably—broken, what guarantee is there in the history of the papal power that there will be no recrudescence of the abuse?

And when Mr. Dawson has explained this issue, there remain further difficulties with which he does not deal. He does not deal with the grim history of the papacy, right down to our own day, as one of the supreme opponents of social change; that is a record pretty accurately symbolized by the excommunication of Lamennais in 1834,[2] and by its willingness to make a concordat with Mussolini, who, after all, represents exactly those anti-Christian habits by the growth of which Mr. Dawson is, and rightly, so alarmed. He does not examine its attitude not merely to the movement of scholarship in general since the French

1 Gerald Brenan, *The Spanish Labyrinth* (Cambridge, 1943), esp. Chap. III.
2 Cf. my *Authority in the Modern State* (London, 1919), Chap. III.

Revolution, its hostility to science, as revealed in its opposition to Darwinism, its dislike of any historical criticism, like that of Duchesne, or Loisy, almost in our own day, or of Döllinger and Kraus, in the nineteenth century, whose results were displeasing to the orthodox tradition, and its fierce resentment, so grimly displayed in its savage treatment of Father Tyrrell, of modernism in the theological field. There have been Roman Catholics, like Marc Sagrier in France, who sought to make their faith the driving force to social betterment. In science and scholarship, the work of Roman Catholic scholars has not seldom been of outstanding value. But it is difficult not to insist that, whatever the qualities of the Roman papacy, it has always sought, even since the French Revolution, to maintain its power to define what men may think and do that it may never jeopardize its power. Often enough, it has failed to achieve its ends; but the outsider will feel, on the record, that the failure is not the outcome of its admission of error, but of the fact that, once its authority in the realm of mind is repudiated, it has no means of imposing it. The Church is not interested in the march of reason unless the end towards which reason marches is the advance of its power.

So that when men like Mr. Dawson plead so persuasively for the return of the unity of Christian civilization, especially for its return under the aegis of the Pope, the outsider is, I think, bound to ask upon what basis, especially in the realm of mind and morals, the return is to be effected, and for whose benefit its restored authority is to be exerted. An examination of the record of the use to which its power was put in the past, and of the methods it was willing to use in the service of that power, does not suggest any title on the part of Mr. Dawson, and of those who think with him, to offer us a world any better than that which existed, say, before the outbreak of the war of 1914; and from that day right down to the autumn of 1943 there has been no clear evidence that the Papacy has sided with democracy against despotism, with reason against unreason, with the masses against their masters; on the contrary, apart from an occasional protest against the regression to barbarism which has had little or no influence upon those to whom it was addressed, the Papacy has either, as with Mussolini, been ready to ally itself with the leaders of the counter-revolution, or, as with Hitlerite Germany, has trodden a labyrinthine path of complicated intrigue which has made it difficult to be sure upon which side it stood in the battle. I invite Mr. Dawson to compare the utterances of an eminent Calvinist, like Karl Barth in Switzerland,[1] or like Reinhold Niebuhr, in the United States of America,[2] with their clarity, their directness, and their vigour, with that tortuous vagueness of all Roman utterances, with their atmosphere of aloofness from the battle even while Rome knows that such aloofness only means that the dictators will have no reason to fear them. If it is unfair to say that the Papacy has been the ally of the dictators; it is, I think, true to say that its hostility has been formal and passive rather than active and determined. It has treated Hitler with a patience and a magnanimity which are in striking contrast with the fury of the attack it has fostered against Soviet Russia.

And even if we suppose—what it is, in fact, supremely difficult even to imagine—that the Papacy arrived at some *modus vivendi* with modern democracy, there then arises a still graver question upon which men of Mr. Dawson's way of faith give us no light. What is left, as history, of the supernatural claims of Christianity, in any of its significant forms, after the two hundred odd years of critical scholarship since the time of Reimarus? We may not accept one particular result or another of its working. What, in any event, it is not seriously open to a scholar to deny is that there is no more ground, except the tradition of Western civilization, for accepting the validity of the postulates upon which the Churches build their rights than there is for accepting those of Mohammedanism or Buddhism; and there is the utmost difficulty in reconciling those postulates with the rights of a reason which examines them upon the assumption

---

1 *A Letter to Great Britain from Switzerland* (London, 1941).
2 *Reflections on the End of an Era* (London, 1937).

that the canons by which testimony is judged sufficient or insufficient are the same in sacred as in secular history.

Anyone, in fact, who seeks to defend the claims of some given Christian Church to belief must fall back on the ancient position of *credo quia impossibile*. And he then steps, at once, into the realm of his right to believe those claims in virtue of an insight which has a power over him he finds irresistible. And, in this realm, it is difficult to see that, for example, the illumination which came to St. Paul has any more authority than that which came to George Fox or to John Bunyan. I am not denying its authority over him to whom it is vouchsafed. I am denying, only, that it can make a rule of conduct, by reason of its authority, over those who have not received its illumination, whether directly, or indirectly. The argument seems to be inescapable that I must either put forward a way of life which is acceptable by reason of its power to prove its right to shape our habits, or, because it puts forward that way of life because behind its plea is a faith which reason is powerless to change. In the first case, the way of life depends upon the normal canons of proof; and I am suggesting that, judged by those canons, the cumulative burden of some two centuries of critical examination is to leave nothing standing of the traditional edifice of Christianity. In the second place, however vivid may be the insight it communicates to its devotees, I am arguing that this does not create a title to authority beyond the men and women who have accepted the dispensation it seeks to impose. For I cannot believe—I do not know Mr. Dawson's view—that my possession of some truths beyond the power of reason to demonstrate can entitle me to enforce their acceptance upon those who see no grounds for believing them to be true. That is to justify persecution; and since I think the outcome of persecution is to breed cruelty and arrogance in the persecutor, and hypocrisy and servility in the persecuted, I am unable to see that the restoration of Christian unity, whether under the aegis of Rome or some other authority, would have any of the results Mr. Dawson so hopefully accepts.

It is, indeed, worth pointing out that, at bottom, it is, if anything, to a miracle that he begs us to look forward. "It is only by the recovery," he writes,[1] "of a dynamic spiritual force which moves the conscience of society more deeply than the material will to power that mankind can be saved from its peril." The terms are vague; but we are, I think, to make them mean that our recovery depends "in the last resort on the existence of a spiritual nucleus of believers who are the bearers of the seed of unity"; and Mr. Dawson is confident of their ultimate triumph because the "powers of the world are blind powers . . . powerless against those higher powers of spiritual knowledge and spiritual understanding which are the essential gifts of the Holy Spirit." [2] But here, of course, we have moved to the realm of a prophecy which claims its authority from its faith in the truth of the Christian revelation and its right to believe that the promises of that revelation will be fulfilled. That is not an argument which will satisfy those who are outside the "spiritual nucleus" of which Mr. Dawson speaks. However much one may agree with him that the problem of attaining a genuine world-order is vital, and that it cannot be solved until power and right are interchangeable terms, we are driven to think that the way to achieve that interchangeability is by proving to our fellows that the values we seek to establish are socially just and intellectually the high road to that society in which ordinary men find that self-fulfilment which gives them the conviction of freedom. And those who form that "spiritual nucleus" of which Mr. Dawson writes so eloquently can in no way do so much to assist in the transvaluation of values which throws open the chance of self-fulfilment to all not by looking back to a revelation which no longer compels, but by looking forward to the chance of aiding with their own hands the building on earth of the celestial city. That is why Blake spoke so great a truth when he said that "desires without deeds breed pestilence"; that is why he was so magnificently right when he sought to build Jerusalem in "England's green and pleasant land."

---

[1] *Op. cit.*, p. 151.
[2] *Ibid.*

I am arguing that this attitude, like that of the poet and the novelist, who use the sense of imagination to interpret our time, is, in fact, an evasion of our problem and not a solution to it. But it is disturbing to note that it is the main attitude, also, of those intellectuals, as with the historian and the economist, whose weapon is scholarship. Orthodox economists have, for the most part, not only assumed the role of the official apologists of the existing economic order, but they have rarely sought to examine that order with the sense that it was historically conditioned, and certain, therefore, to be the subject of change. They spoke of its "laws" less as generalizations of particular sets of circumstances which were always in a state of flux than as though they were the imperatives of a permanent sovereign whose will it was the duty of his subjects to obey without question. This has resulted in their organizing for their discussions a universe of concepts in which the definitions and postulates determined the real character of the theorems at which they arrived. "The orthodox economists," writes Mrs. Robinson,[1] "have been much preoccupied with elegant elaborations of minor problems, which distract the attention of their pupils from the uncongenial realities of the modern world, and the development of abstract argument has run far ahead of any possibility of empirical verification. Marx's intellectual tools are far cruder, but his sense of reality is far stronger, and his argument towers above their intricate constructions in rough and gloomy grandeur." The economists, in the years between the wars, were playing, no doubt not seldom with great skill and finesse, an intricate game in which the main objective seemed to be an evasion of the obligation to ask the right questions lest they should receive the right answers. Few things better illustrate the pathos of their situation than the way in which, during the great depression, they were continually predicting that prosperity was round the corner save the attitude of that school of thought which, because it believed on *a priori* grounds that it was impossible to plan, did not think it either necessary or desirable to examine in the

---

1 Joan M. Robinson, *An Essay on Marxian Economics* (London, 1942), p. 3.

Soviet Union that great planning experiment which, when war actually came, made possible the avoidance of a new dark age.

"It is impossible," wrote Trotsky, "to play with history." That is the lesson which but few of the intellectuals who used the tools of scholarship seemed willing to learn between 1919 and 1939. Society had set in motion certain forces; either their dynamic had to be arrested, or they had to move to their predestined end. The forces it was the business of the economist and the historian to understand they seemed, with but rare exceptions, only too anxious to neglect. One has only to examine the vast majority of the works published by scholars in these fields during these years to see how little they were set in the perspective to which events compelled them. What was in question was the traditional foundation of the state-authority, its economic imperatives, its political character, the behaviour it exacted from those from whom it sought to compel obedience. Everyone knew, at least from the time of Mussolini's seizure of power, that the world had entered into an epoch of crisis which, if it did not make all things new, at least gave new horizons to every ancient issue. Yet the main bulk of work by economists and historians assumed the validity of the old categories, built upon the idea that progress is both permanent and inevitable, accepted a hedonistic calculus which few philosophers and no psychologists were any longer prepared to defend, and inferred therefrom that the rationality of man is the equality in his spirit which gives its chief character to his actions.

It is difficult, in fact, to examine the general nature of scholarship in these years—I am not, of course, denying that there are outstanding and remarkable exceptions—without the conviction that its basic framework was defined less in relation to the problem it was urgent to solve than because of its capacity to satisfy a certain result which the intellectuals were anxious to approve. It is easy to understand why a Whig like Macaulay, to whom the very idea of universal suffrage was detestable, could write of the Revolution of 1688 in terms of epic eulogy; its real consequence, after all, was to bring the middle class to power, and Macaulay considered the middle class "the natural representative of the human race." It is easy, again, to see why, in the grim aftermath of the Napoleonic wars, Ricardo and his school could outline an economic theory which seemed to despair of any prospect of generally advancing welfare. What is impossible to understand is the attitude of the historian three-quarters of a century after Macaulay who denies all his premises of thought, in the light of his experience of their outcome, and yet begins, in the light of that denial, ingeniously to refine away the case for democracy to which his analysis leads. It is still more impossible to understand the attitude of the economist who explains the grounds upon which the pessimism of Ricardo may be countered and then proceeds to emphasize the futility of exactly the institutions and discoveries, both social and technological, out of which the grounds for optimism have already emerged.

It is not, I think, too much to say of the main body of humanistic scholarship in the inter-war years that it largely lacked a wisdom that was in any serious degree proportionate to its massive learning. Partly, I think, that lack of wisdom was the outcome of excessive specialization, and partly of the cult of "impartiality" by the scholar; by which last was really meant that he sought, if he possibly could, to make his inquiries irrelevant to the struggle upon which his age had embarked. The scholars of Europe and America were moving into that atmosphere of mind so superbly described by the great Russian novelists in the seventy-five years before 1917. They were beseeched, above all in the universities, to answer questions which, if they could, they steadfastly refused to ask. They sought confinement in an ivory tower in which they could shut out the crude and angry problems of the real world lest, in facing them, they discovered that their ivory tower was, in fact, a beleaguered fortress they would be called upon to defend.

The abyss which separates the intellectuals of the main world of scholarship, above all in the academic world, from the main problems of their time is as grave in its implications as it is wide in its extent. In the seventeenth century, philosophers like Descartes and Hobbes, Spinoza and Locke, scientists like Galileo and Newton and Leibniz, shaped in supreme measure the mental climate of their time. On six separate occasions Addison cites Locke in the *Spectator* as one whose glory is a national possession; and even Bishop Warburton, who had no fondness for a rival to his glory, could speak of him as "the honour of this age and the instructor of the future" nearly a generation after Locke's death. In the eighteenth century the house of Voltaire at Ferney is almost a European shrine; and there are few unhappy souls in any Western country who do not turn to Rousseau for aid and counsel as though to a major prophet to whom had been confined the secrets of the universe. In the nineteenth century, the writings of Carlyle and Ruskin, of Dickens and the younger Mill, of Renan and Michelet, of Tolstoy and Whitman, swept over the spaces of the world. Everyone knows that even in the log cabins of the American frontier, the traveller would find, apart from the Bible and Shakespeare, a well-thumbed copy of Macaulay's *Essays*. Up to some such time as the years between the death of Matthew Arnold and the death of William Morris, the labours of the scholar played their part in giving its definitive character to the mental climate in which the masses lived and thought and felt. For almost the four centuries from the day when Luther pinned his ninety-five theses to the door of the Cathedral at Wittenberg the scholar's humanism was, even if he was unconscious of it, an integral element in shaping the quality of the common man's life.

But, in the last half-century in general, and in the last twenty-five years in particular, the divorce between scholarship and life has been as striking as in the case of poetry and the novel. The scholar no longer writes except for other scholars. He has developed specialization to a degree which deprives his work of meaning for, almost of the power to be read by, the ordinary cultivated person. And it is difficult not to feel that no small part of this specialization is really less inherent in the subject-matter than in the scholar's desire to avoid large, general issues, and especially those amongst them which seem relevant to the crisis of our time. Great creative work in the humanistic field, the desire to tackle the big subject, the confidence which embarks upon the massive generalization, these depend, individual exceptions apart, upon a sense of security in the society; and when that sense of security is absent, the will to attempt great creative work is likely to be absent, too. For no scholar can do great creative work without plunging into vital controversy, and, if he feels insecure, it is only too likely that he will either avoid the issue which defines his social outlook, or, alternatively, seek to maintain a secure position by writing what will not provoke offence from those in power, or even win approval from them. So that just as imaginative literature in our time, while it may be willing to denounce, has rarely been willing to defy, and has mostly, as I have said, looked for a cul-de-sac in which to take refuge, so, the literature of scholarship has turned from the high road lest its practitioners find that they are led to challenge the existing order. The Whig school of history, for example, may have refused to find any place in its conception for a democracy which passed the frontiers of property; but it did believe profoundly in the rule of law, and it had, on its economic side, a dislike of privilege and monopoly which made it, on the whole, the enemy of reaction in its day. Those who reject its scheme of values in favour of a right-wing attitude tend increasingly to an implicit *Realpolitik* which defends the end successfully attained without paying regard to the way in which it is attained.

This attitude comes out with startling clarity in the field of history; and I may perhaps illustrate its consequences by some examples from the study of British and American work. At the close of the liberal epoch which was terminated by the war of 1914, Mr. and Mrs. Hammond had begun to publish the remarkable series of studies of the Industrial Revolution and its aftermath, the Chartist Movement, in which they dissected, with a sensitive and profound understanding, the bill of psychological costs which the workers had to pay for the massive economic triumph of the British plutocracy. Until the end of the war, and perhaps even into the first years of the peace of Versailles, their books were received with enthusiasm by the professional critics, and they undoubtedly played their part in defining that new sense of self-consciousness which made possible the organization of the Labour Party in 1918. No one was quite sure what the defeat of Germany would mean; and most shrewd observers recognized that the Russian Revolution was bound to reopen that question of the place of the worker in society which had been decided in favour of privilege in 1848. So long as the impact of the Russian Revolution was uncertain, historians were prepared to recognize the general validity of the Hammonds' thesis. But once it became clear that Bolshevism could be confined within the Russian frontiers, there developed what can only be called a counter-revolution in British historiography, which culminated in the general acceptance of Sir J. H. Clapham's *An Economic History of Modern Britain* as the almost official expression of the findings of scholarship about the period with which Mr. and Mrs. Hammond had been mainly concerned.

I do not need for one moment to deny the vast researches upon which Sir John Clapham's book is built, nor the great skill with which they are organized into a general pattern. My interest is in the unconscious assumptions which underlie Sir John's narrative. It is significant, first, that the authorities upon which he chiefly relies are Government reports, and the files of newspapers like the *Times* or journals like the *Economist*.[1] The material, so to say, from which the pattern is woven is that provided by the men who conquered or their half-official agents like Bagehot. And since, in the outcome, there emerges a Britain whose economic supremacy in 1914 no other power was able or willing successfully to challenge, Sir John Clapham does not even consider it necessary to discuss the argument which underlay Mr. and Mrs. Hammond's eloquent indictment of the first part of the nineteenth century. The moral of his three volumes appears to be the futility of contemplating the tragedy embodied

1 Cf. the very illuminating speech made by Mr. Herbert Morrison at the Centenary lunch of the *Economist* and published in the pamphlet reporting the occasion.

in the individual agony of millions of Stephen Blackpools or the individual complacency of hundreds of Gradgrinds and Bounderbys since the outcome of the innumerable Coketowns that they built is not only success in war, but a vastly increased national wealth and a higher standard of living for nearly every economic group in the community. Sir John Clapham's *History* may be not unfairly termed the record of the triumph of what Carlyle called the cash-nexus as the sole way in which the economic relations of men are organized. It does not occur to him to inquire whether the triumph was in fact already over when he was writing, or that a society cannot seriously claim a final victory over a tragic destiny when the social comment on the cash-nexus is the fierce indignation of *Past and Present,* the well-bred irony of *Culture and Anarchy,* or the hopeless disillusion of *Jude the Obscure.* The historian of English economic development in the nineteenth century ignores these things because they involve the need to apply a scheme of values incapable of reduction into terms of money. The conclusion is inferred rather than emphasized that justice has triumphed in the Britain of the post-Napoleonic period, and that the basis of the triumph is the achievement of private enterprise. It is assumed that the concentration both of riches and authority in a small fragment of the population is the necessary condition of capital accumulation; and Sir John Clapham averts his eyes from the grim spectacle in which that accumulation by the savings of a small number of individuals is purchased by depriving the masses of access to the cultural heritage of the British nation and condemning the vast majority to a life in which there is rarely security and seldom more than a dull routine of effort in work mitigated by a leisure in which the proportion is small which can hope to use it in a creative way. That the proper comment on the whole narrative is its end in a ghastly conflict even the victory in which its leaders did not know how to use so that the peace it ushers in is merely the prelude to a second and more terrible conflict does not occur to the historian. Like the contemporary ecclesiastic, having excluded a moral judgment on the immediate scene from the ambit of his task, he does not even realize that the history he is writing is no more than the verdict of the class that has conquered upon the outcome of their effort.

American historiography has undergone something akin to a renaissance since the inspiration was given it by F. J. Turner's great essay on the frontier to deal with the interaction of men and things, instead of being satisfied with history as a system of ideas born, Minerva-like, in the brain of some great statesman. Above all since 1913, when Charles Beard published his classic study [1] of the men who made the American Constitution, there has been a realism in American historical writing, a willingness to face, in all its implications, the grim consequences of a society in which classes fight with passion for the possession of the state-power which, though it may have been equalled, even surpassed, by one of half a dozen supreme European masters of the historian's art, Maitland in England, for example, or Pirenne in Belgium, or Troeltsch in Germany, or in De Sanctis' masterpiece upon the history of Italian literature, has, in its collective level, had a quality of freedom and imagination which no other country has rivalled. Yet, despite individual contributions of high distinction, above all, perhaps, those of Charles and Mary Beard in their *Rise of American Civilization,* or of Vernon Parrington, in his *Main Currents in American Thought,* one can detect in the period after Harding arrived at the Presidency a slow erosion of the earlier realism which it is not, I think, unfair to attribute to the growing fear of the organized masses. In part, this can be seen in the treatment of the American War of Independence; there is a tendency, as in the study of its causes by the late Professor Van Tyne,[2] to assume that there was relatively little to choose between the parties to the conflict. It is seen, even more strikingly, in the biographies officially written for McClellan and Cleveland, for Hamilton Fish and Elihu Root and John D. Rockefeller. We move, as it were, from the angry mood

---

1 *Economic Interpretation of the Constitution* (New York, 1913).

2 Claude H. Van Tyne, *The Causes of the War of Independence* (1922).

of Henry Demarest Lloyd's *Wealth Against Commonwealth* (1884), in which the little man speaks out with passion against the growing sovereignty of the great corporation, from the bitter indignation of Gustavus Myers' *History of the Great American Fortunes* (1907) to a new era in which what is regarded as important is that Marshall, as in Beveridge's biography,[1] made America secure for business men against the plea of Jeffersonian democracy, or, as in Ulrich B. Phillips' study of slavery in the South,[2] that, so to say, Lord Acton was broadly right when "he broke his heart over the surrender of Lee." Men like Altgeld, incidents like the Haymarket riots, had to wait for reasonable treatment until the great depression, which began in 1929, resulted in the experiments of the New Deal from 1933. And even then, when the outbreak of war, as a result of Pearl Harbor, resulted in the return to full employment, historians of the high distinction of Louis Hacker, who had, in the years of crisis, explained with passion the bankruptcy of traditional Americanism,[3] were willing to remake their assumptions of the earlier period, and narrate, upon a basis which Sir John Clapham would have accepted eagerly, an American history in which the hero was the millionaire adventurer who had not only been the villain of the earlier volumes,[4] but had been grimly exposed for the price the United States had paid for his adventurism in a mass of government inquiries and specialist monographs.[5] Just as the war of 1914 transformed the main supporters of Wilsonian liberalism into the ardent advocates of a *laissez-faire* society, so the vistas opened by the recognition, in 1941, of the immense influence Russia was likely to exert, began to recreate in the United States an economic nationalism which enlisted the scholars who had, before that date, predicted with some equanimity the de-

1 Albert J. Beveridge, *Life of John Marshall* (Boston, 1919).

2 *American Negro Slavery* (New York, 1918).

3 Cf. his *The United States since 1865* and *American Problems of Today* (1938) with his *Triumph of American Capitalism* (1940).

4 A. A. Berle, Jr. and G. C. Means, *The Modern Corporation and Private Property* (1932); A. R. Burns, *The Decline of Competition* (1936).

5 Cf. the Monographs of the National Resources Committee, above all, the remarkable essay of B. J. Stein on the frustration of science.

cline of American capitalism, into enthusiastic advocates of its claim to a destiny manifestly more splendid than anything to which the old world could look forward.[1]

It would not be difficult to show that what is true of American historical writing has been true also in the fields of economics and sociology. With, as always, important individual exceptions, of which, in the first, the outstanding figure is Thorstein Veblen, and, in the second, that remarkable figure in American jurisprudence, Mr. Justice Brandeis, any close examination of these fields of scholarship in the United States exhibits their main exponents as devoted to the defence of existing conditions. In an obviously revolutionary age, it was rare to find, outside the ranks of the professional advocates of revolution, any important thinker who insisted on the need in the United States for fundamental change. Yet it was not less obvious in the United States than in Europe that when a situation had been reached where free immigration was prohibited, and only war could create a condition of full employment, there was a clear need for fundamental change. Since change of this character is achieved either by consent or else by revolution, it became difficult not to conclude that, if the scholars were broadly united in opposing the view that fundamental change should be effected by consent, the situation was being created in which, when peace came, the stage would, no doubt slowly, be set for a drama in which a violent solution of the problem of the play was bound to be the outcome.

The American scholar who handled these issues was partly blinded, I suspect, by his natural desire to win the war, and partly misled by his misinterpretation of the significance of American economic power. The peaceful solution of class differences can, after all, be achieved by one of two ways only. Either it is effected by the existence, in some given society, of a power continuously to distribute well-being from the apex to

---

[1] Cf. Lewis Corey, *The Decline of American Capitalism* (1934), and John Chamberlain's *Farewell to Reform* (1932) with their books and articles published after the beginning of the second World War.

the base of the social pyramid. That was the happy condition of the United States until some such period as the decade after the closing of the frontier. Or it can be effected, though far more rarely, because the man of letters, be he poet or critic, philosopher or novelist, has deep sympathy with the new aspirations and a conscience which compels him to act upon his sympathy. In the latter event, it is obviously the duty of the thinker, whether he cultivates the field of imaginative literature or the field of scholarship, to find the means whereby he correlates the vague aspirations of the masses into the coherence of a practical programme. The task of the thinker is to clear the ground for action which creates hope and exhilaration in the common man. It is not enough for him merely to photograph, as it were, in the manner of novelists like James T. Farrell, the bitter life of the masses. It is not even enough for the eminent poet, like Archibald MacLeish, for example, to ask for better things for the masses. Nor does the solution come when a famous philosopher, like John Dewey, compiles a fairly concrete list of desirable reforms. All of this America had in the springtime of New England; all of this, also, Great Britain had when the major emphasis of the great Victorians gave specific form and content to mass-desire. And all of this, it may be added, was done with superb insight by the French *philosophes* in the eighteenth century, by the early socialists of Europe before 1848, and by the Russian revolutionaries in the period between the departure of Herzen for Europe and the Revolution of October.

The real sympathy lies in the union of the intellectual and the masses, as between Sam Adams and the Committees of Correspondence, between Jefferson and the early republicans, between Marx and Engels and the European socialist movement out of which the First International was born, between Lenin in exile and the Bolshevik party in Russia, and in a smaller way, perhaps less successfully, between Sidney and Beatrice Webb and the British Labour movement in the generation before the collapse of 1931. The union may not succeed; the scale of antagonism and power on the other side may be too great to permit of its success. I am only certain that the responsibility of the intellectual who sees the drift of his time towards the abyss is to mitigate its dangers by seeking, through the profundity of his alliance with the masses, to make their dreams and hopes seem practicable and legitimate. To stand apart from the danger as a neutral, even more, to lend his aid, when he has awareness of it, to the oligarchy in power, is a supreme betrayal of his function. This is what Trotsky really meant when he said we must understand that it is impossible to play with history. The intellectuals may postpone catastrophe; the evidence is overwhelming that they cannot prevent it even if they succeed in postponing it. But there is no limit to the service they can render to society when, aware of the danger, they insist upon using their insight and imagination to prevent its translation into the habits of a new dark age. It was the failure of the Italian intellectuals to insist upon this use that allowed Mussolini to steal into power. It was the failure of the German intellectuals which permitted Hitler to establish his ugly empire. It was the failure of the French intellectuals, after 1919, which created the conditions out of which France was overthrown in 1940. Let us not deceive ourselves into the belief that the conditions in Britain and the United States are different. The intellectuals, in both countries, are not likely to play any great part in the winning of the war. But they will play an immense part in the winning of the peace on the one vital condition that they recognize the depth of their responsibility for defining the political problems we shall then confront.

The meaning of that responsibility we can hardly mistake after these grim years of war. It means their obligation to ally themselves with the future that is struggling to be born and not with the past that is dying before our eyes. It means their determination to take their stand alongside the masses who are the victims of an outworn economic and political system, and not to lend their aid to the privileged few whose one ambition is the preservation of Heartbreak House. It is not enough for them to profess the acceptance of the Christian ethic. In its operation, that ethic has accommodated itself to slavery at its ugliest, to capitalism in its most ruthless form, to every war that has been waged since Constantine made Christianity the official religion of the Empire. "The same nice people, the same utter futility," writes Mr. Bernard Shaw. "The nice people could read; some of them could write; and they were the only repositories of culture who had social opportunities of contact with our politicians, administrators, and newspaper proprietors. But they shrank from that contact. They hated politics. They did not wish to realize Utopia for the common people: they wished to realize their favourite fictions and poems in their own lives; and, when they could, they lived without scruple on incomes they had done nothing to earn. . . . They took the only part of our society in which there was leisure for high culture, and made it an economic, political, and as far as practicable, a moral vacuum; and as Nature, abhorring the vacuum, immediately filled it up with sex, and with all sorts of refined pleasures, it was a very delightful place at its best for moments of relaxation. In other moments it was disastrous. For Prime Ministers and their like, it was a veritable Capua." [1]

This is not the language of rhetorical exaggeration, but of sober common sense. Just as the Christian Church adapted itself, with an occasional moment of protest or of anguish, to the claims of that worldly materialism it had come to deny, from whose results, indeed, it had been born, so the intellectuals, whether as poets or novelists, whether as historians or philosophers, with rare exceptions ignored the meaning of the world it was their business to assist in changing in the hope that their claims to security and comfort might be accepted by those in whose power they thought it lay to dispense such satisfactions. So that even when, like Mr. Galsworthy, they were dismayed at the strident barbarism of the successful *bourgeoisie,* they remained aloof from politics; they would not have known how to act politically even if they had entered the arena. Some of them, indeed, quite frankly turned their backs on life, in the firm

1 G. B. Shaw, *Collected Works* (1930), Vol. 15, Preface to *Heartbreak House,* p. 4.

conviction that the return of nature was a truth from the results of which they were exempted. And in the elegant refinement of a Chelsea studio, or the golden backwater of an Oxford college, they comforted themselves with the reflection that since the life of the masses was an ugly thing, beauty must be a perception limited to the *élite,* to whom, naturally, they were convinced that they belonged.

The ugliness which made up the life of the masses, the mean houses, the semi-starvation, the constant insecurity of employment, the low wages and the long hours, the leisure which was either dulled by fatigue, or deprived of grace by the loudness of its crudity, all this, as they saw, made for a low standard of public taste in all matters with which the arts were concerned. So that it was inevitable, they told themselves, that the crowd should prefer jazz to Beethoven, W. P. Frith's *Derby Day* to Cézanne's self-portrait, the verses of Edgar Guest to the sonnets of Shakespeare, *Gone with the Wind* to *Anna Karenina.* And, on the assumption of this inevitability, the intellectual ceased to address the masses at all, and concerned himself only with debates mainly confined to other intellectuals. The result was the simple one that the intellectuals, who might have aided those who sought to renovate the foundations of society, ceased to be concerned with either the interest or the importance of this renovation, and became an appendage of the ruling class. It was the outcome of this relationship that, in ever increasing degree, they not only shared the general standards of the ruling class, but omitted to notice, in their desire to emulate those standards, that their price was a war between both nations and classes which it was increasingly impossible to postpone. In the degree that they cut themselves off from the popular movement, they did not understand that they deprived it of the environment in which the minds and hearts of the masses could develop cultivation and discipline. They left anger to be ignorant which they might have made creative had they sought to give it knowledge. But they were as aloof from the peasant in the village or the artisan in the factory as the fantastic creatures who in Chekhov and Turgenev, in Tolstoy and Dostoevski, mistook the elaborate ballet they performed in the waste land for the brave new world in which men acclaimed either the uniqueness of the beauty they created or the significance of the massive learning they amassed. They failed to see that to the solid *bourgeoisie* they had meaning only as a decoration which won an occasional glance, and that to the masses they were largely devoid of meaning because they had abandoned that relation between the artist and the common man which made the latter feel Byron's death as a personal loss or recognize humbly in Dickens a giant who played with the stars.

When the Church and the intellectuals have abandoned truth for power, and rejected the public joy of mutual communication for the private pleasure of whispering secrets to a chosen band, it is not remarkable that there should not only be violent conflict, but also that the discovery of a meaning in that conflict should be a task even more deadly than the cost of fighting. For a literature, whether of imagination or of scholarship, that is divorced from the society in which it is expressed has lost that power to guide life towards the heights which is, after all, its supreme function. We have been pretending to ourselves for something like forty years now that the artist has no concern with politics, that his task is imaginative creation which must transcend the temporary issues about which politicians quarrel so futilely in the market-place. Yet, if we are honest with ourselves, we know that there is a profound political purpose in some of the greatest works of imaginative creation, and, even more, that the power to produce them depends upon a mental and moral climate in the society the existence of which itself raises some of the profoundest political questions.

I do not mean to say that the great writer or the great scholar must serve his apprenticeship to art by addressing envelopes in the committee room of his party; I do not even suggest that he will necessarily benefit from playing an active role in politics, though it is remarkable how large a proportion of the most valuable political literature has been written by men who knew their subject, like Machiavelli and Burke, like Marx and Lenin, from first-hand experience of its working. I am concerned with the less dramatic argument that the intellectual is a citizen as well as a private person, and that the literature of an age will never be helpful to that age, will rarely, even, be great literature, if the intellectual turns his back upon the outstanding problems it confronts. I do not mean that the poet must understand the theory of the trade cycle or that a novelist without a programme of public works is bound to write bad novels if there is a large percentage of unemployed. But I do mean that in an age which, like our own, is shaken to its foundations, the intellectuals must have a sense of the urgency of the times if their work is to be creative. They cannot, as a group in society, deliberately evade an interest in what is often a matter of life and death for the masses, and then hope, in what they do as intellectuals, to seem significant to the masses. When a democracy so operates that its leading intellectuals, Byron or Dickens, Scott or Balzac, somehow seem closely integrated with what is essential in its life, they are performing the functions to which, as intellectuals, they are called. Their minds and hearts are likely to effect the thought and the sentiment of their contemporaries in a decisive way; they are a safeguard against that danger which, just after the Easter Rebellion in Dublin, Mr. George Russell warned his fellow-countrymen might easily lead them astray—the temptation to confound the easy job of feeling deeply about things with the far more difficult job of thinking seriously about them.[1]

But when the intellectuals, whether they be Henry James in one generation, or Mr. T. S. Eliot in its successor, stand aloof from all the problems by which their time is troubled, even more, when they concentrate their main attention upon problems of an entirely different order, they are in fact deserting the main task to which they are called, and what they have to say will have little influence upon the predominant temper of their age. They may address a small clique who find in their pro-

[1] Æ, *The National Being* (Dublin, 1916), p. 6. The next ten pages are a superb illustration of the point I am trying to make.

nouncements truths of the first importance; but unless it happens—and it is rare that it will happen—that the clique which they address disposes of the state-power, they are really standing apart from the intellectuals' function of giving their fellow-citizens counsel on the vital issues they have to solve. And it is, of course, pretty certain that if they decline to perform this function the masses will look elsewhere for that counsel. What they will get is more than likely to come from men who speak from interest rather than from conviction. And counsel built on interest is, almost always, prejudiced towards the maintenance of a superstition which, however glowing the prospectus it offers, will be found on ultimate examination to be an indirect method of saving some special privilege which fears the light of day. We have only to compare the "unchangeable" programme of the Nazis, of 1924, with the reality the German people received when Hitler came to power, or to contrast the Fascist promise with the Fascist fact, to see what occurs in a society when the major issues of the age are neglected by its thinkers out of a fear that they may become involved in controversy.

A world which, like ours, is almost overwhelmed by the strain of the crisis through which it is passing is bound to look for recovery to its priests and prophets not less than to its rulers. And no duty the two former can fulfil is more urgent than to concentrate the attention of the masses upon the central issues of the crisis, and to persuade them, if they can, to confront those issues in rational terms. From this, I think, it follows that the wider the formal dispersion of political power, the more urgent is the need for intellectual leadership because the more dangerous are likely to be the consequences of what I have called superstition. In a period like ours, when few men can find the familiar landmarks by which they moved securely on their way, fear tends to beget political passion, and we are all caught in the grip of an emotional instability which makes the false prophet difficult to distinguish from the real. And once the false prophet gets a hold upon the social mind, the danger is overwhelming that persuasion will give way to force, and that he will suspend those processes of intellectual liberation by which a people is restored to sanity.

It need not be restored; the decay may become so deeply embedded in the roots of its life that recovery is no longer open to it. Civilizations have perished before in history; and anyone who examines their destruction will find, I think, that one, at least, of its most fundamental causes is that superstition has taken so firm a hold upon the mind of the nation that it no longer possesses within itself the means whereby the authority of reason can effect a restoration of unity. It then ceases to be at one with itself about the great ends of life; and, like the Greek city-states, and the Roman Empire, the external challenge merely completes an inner defeat that has already been accomplished. That, in our own day, was the case with France; its intellectuals had betrayed it before its generals courted the opportunity of surrender. They had betrayed it because they refused to make its people understand the issues by which it was confronted in the inter-war years. Men like Maurras thought less of the idea of France, as that idea had been shaped by events like those of 1789 upon which there can be no going back, than of the idea of a France which could only be achieved by making the history of one hundred and fifty years a thing of futility. Maurras and his colleagues of the *Action Française* were guilty of that treason which refuses guidance to the nation on the real crisis in which it is involved in order to compel attention to issues which, collectively, constitute exactly what I have called a superstition. For while he and his school of thought were diverting the energies of the people from the serious problem of property to the inherently frivolous issue of the monarchical principle, the divisions he created were utilized by the *Comité des Forges* and the Cagoulards to put Laval in power, under the shadow of Pétain's once great name, as the instrument of Hitler. The real betrayal of which men like Maurras were guilty is that they sacrificed France to its enemies for the sake of vested interests the nature of which they never attempted to reveal. And if it be said that Maurras had never the thought of inflicting upon the

French masses a defeat so terrible or sufferings so profound, the answer is that once he had set the crisis in France in the incredible proportions upon which he lavished so much care, the objective result which followed in 1940 was logically inherent in his substitution of superstition for reason.

XI

From Epicurus to the Empire

BY A strange coincidence, the same confusion of superstition with reason which accompanied the fall of France accompanied, in ancient Rome, the notion of that freedom and dignity which were lost when the Republic gave place to the Empire. It was, Mr. J. M. Robertson has said,[1] "the fatal maxim of ancient scepticism that religion is a necessary restraint upon the multitude." There was a brief period in the history of the Republic when it seemed as though the growth of influence of the Epicurean philosophy would act as a means of liberating men's minds. For it banished the fear of death; it heaped contempt upon the illusion that the anger of the gods was visited upon men in the shape of thunder and lightning, storm and disease. Epicurus had called upon men to renounce that acquisitive society which turned what might have been a happy world into a gigantic prison. If men would but study nature and live by the practice of friendship, there would be open to them a new earth in which they might lead the life of gods. For Epicurus, the wider the hold of truth upon men's minds, the greater their emancipation from the grim superstition of the traditional religion, the less would it be necessary to fight for security as the beast, haunted by fear, lives in the jungle. To give to the masses the knowledge which science makes possible is to achieve for all the "blessedness of the complete life."

We know that there was at any rate a brief period in which the doctrines of Epicurus gained numerous disciples and that he himself was held in high honour. But he was preaching the evil of acquisitiveness and the need to free the masses from the thraldom of superstition to a society racked by civil dissension

[1] *A History of Free Thought in the Nineteenth Century*, Vol. 1, p. 135.

in which the ruling class thought of religion as one of the most vital means by which the poor could be held in subjection. To the Roman Senate the gospel that it was desirable to free the poor from servitude, and enable them to think for themselves was, like the socialism of Jaurès and Blum to Maurras and his disciples, to overturn the foundations of social order. We hear in the pages of Polybius, who in his seventeen years as a hostage in Rome learned to reflect the habits of mind of that ruling class whose methods he so greatly admired, why the freedom Epicurus had proposed was so fiercely rejected. "I venture to assert," wrote Polybius, "that what most of mankind holds in contempt is the foundation of Roman greatness, namely superstition. This factor has been introduced into every aspect of their private and public life, with every artifice to awe the imagination, in a degree upon which it is impossible to improve. Possibly, many will be at a loss to understand this policy; in my view, it has been done to impress the masses. If a state were possible in which all the citizens were philosophers, maybe we could dispense with such methods. But in every state the masses are unstable, full of lawless desires, of irrational anger, and violent passion. So that we can do no more than hold them restrained by fears of the unseen, and similar shams. It was not for nought, but of set purpose, that the men of old introduced to the masses ideas about the gods, and theories of the life to come. Ours is the folly and the recklessness who attempt to dispel these illusions." [1]

Polybius is one of the supreme historians of the ancient world. He is not himself a victim of the superstitions the imposition of which upon the masses he so strongly recommends. Like Plato, he defends the "noble lie" because he assumes that the capacity for reason and virtue is limited to a small leisured class. He is afraid that if the power of superstition is destroyed, the masses will be unwilling to accept the burden of that acquisitive society in which the leisure of the few is a privilege created by the toil of the many. He is dismayed by the willingness of the Epicureans,

---

1 Polybius, *Histories,* VI, 56.

who are prepared to regard the masses as fit for enlightenment, to destroy the values which preserve the traditional oligarchy of the ancient world. He therefore accepts the technique of indoctrination in superstition as the only way in which the privileges of the Roman oligarchy can be preserved. He has nothing, for instance, of that overmastering passion we find in Lucretius against a world in which the "life of man lies foul to see and grovelling upon the earth, crushed by the weight of religion." For Lucretius, the nobility of the Epicurean dream is that it was the first great attack on a popular state-cult by which the masses are held in subjection to the few by the power of a superstitious faith backed by the state-authority. He seeks, like his master, to set them free from the chains of a religious slavery which is the basis upon which a social slavery is also built. And it is evident from a mass of contemporary testimony that the rational appeal of this liberating doctrine has a great hold upon the populace; that is evident, for example, by the anger and contempt with which Cicero treats it. And it is clear, too, that when Stoicism, in its Roman phase, has lost the revolutionary verve with which it had begun, and is adapted to the needs of the Roman oligarchy, it triumphs over the effort of the Epicureans to popularize knowledge, and release men from the trammels of superstition. The "noble lie," which keeps the truth from the masses, is based on what Fowler calls the "statesmanlike instinct" of men like Cicero whose main object is to maintain the hold of a system of ideas, unacceptable in private to a man of his sophisticated intelligence, which enables the masses to be exploited in the interest of an historic privilege which they do not believe can hold its ground on other terms. "What chance," asked Varro, "had poor ignorant men of escaping the combined deceit both of the devils and of the leading men of the state." The answer is, of course, no chance at all. For, as St. Augustine had seen in quoting Varro, the hostility of paganism to the poor was of its essence; the state protects the old gods in the interest of the rich.[1] On the pagan altar, Greek and Roman intel-

---

[1] *City of God*, Bk. IV, Chap. 36.

lectual alike sacrificed truth and freedom lest, as they were widely shared, they might injure the oligarchy of traditional privilege.

No doubt, at one stage, there were thinkers who were ashamed of, or regretful at, the decision that was made. The goodwill shown by Pericles to Anaxagoras, which almost resulted in his overthrow, is a deliberate patronage extended to the new science; and we may reasonably infer from the proud eulogy of Prometheus by Aeschylus, especially in contrast with the contempt he pours upon the subservient Oceanus, that the poet was well aware of what was involved in the decision.[1] It emerges with passion in the plays of Euripides; himself the personal friend of Anaxagoras, something of the magic of the new knowledge became a living part of his song. But it is obvious from the *Clouds* of Aristophanes, and the poems of Pindar, himself almost exactly a contemporary of Aeschylus, that the political dangers of the experimental temper which Ionian philosophy was making popular were becoming ever more clear. If the people are permitted to doubt the gods, how much more will they be inclined to doubt the claims of their human masters to privilege and power? That is, surely, the secret which underlies the willingness of Plato that the "noble lie" shall give stability to the state. However ardent his eulogy of truth, it is still something beyond the grasp of ordinary men. So that Plato is content to ask that the citizen be instructed to identify virtue with obedience to the law; and in the tenth book of his *Laws* he is emphatic that the ancient faith must be perpetuated because, otherwise, all things will be brought into question. The old gods are to safeguard the commonwealth against doubts which, if they are permitted to grow, may break up the class character of the state upon which privilege is based. That this is, in fact, what Plato was urging upon his contemporaries is clear from a passage in

---

[1] G. G. M. Thomson's remarkable introduction to his edition of *Prometheus Vinctus* (1932). There is much that is illuminating on the organized use of religion for reactionary purposes in Thomas Whitaker, *Priests, Philosophers and Kings* (London, 1911), a book which, if I may say so, has never had the recognition it deserves.

the *Metaphysics*[1] in which Aristotle, so much the greatest of his pupils, speaks of the "myths that have been invented to persuade the multitude, because of their value for social custom and the public good." The masses are not permitted to see behind the veil; it is, in Burke's phrase, their business "to venerate where they are unable presently to comprehend." And the vast mythology of the official creed is a construction maintained in the interest of the vested privileges of an aristocratic society.

The aristocracy won; the intellectuals deserted the cause of truth for fear that the growth of popular knowledge might intensify that civil conflict which the inequalities of the ancient world so constantly begot. But we must not forget an indirect result of this victory and the desertion that was its basis. The fatal maxim, as J. M. Robertson called it, which I have already quoted, that religion is a necessary restraint upon the masses, brought with it another consequence of grievous import. It meant, as he said, "everywhere that, in the last resort, the unenlightened multitude became a restraint upon reason and free thought." In the effort, in a word, to preserve their privileges, the means of thinking became the weapon of a class the use of which is forbidden to those excluded from its confines. The outcome is the evolution of a proletariat which is not merely forbidden to seek an understanding of the universe, but has even lost the desire to seek that understanding. And because even a proletariat must have some compensation for the illusions to which it is conditioned, the state must organize on its behalf the means of satisfying the passionate superstitions engendered among the great mass of its citizens. When religion, as a weapon of the governing class, crushes the dignity of manhood out of the common people, it makes their hold of superstition a technique whereby a barrier is erected in the way even of desirable change. The Rome that Sallust depicts for us has already begun to lose that inner integrity which might have preserved its liberties. The Republic gives way to the Empire for that simplest of all reasons that its masses have for long

[1] XII, 8, 13, 1074b.

ceased to understand the secret of freedom. It watches the Senate replaced by the Emperor with no question in its mind because it has been so long taught that it is an evil thing to question the verdict of constituted authority. It has become as evil for the *proles* to doubt the validity of imperial power as it has been for him, over centuries, to doubt the truth embodied in the faith of his gods among whom each emperor is himself shortly to be numbered. The mind of the masses is thus disciplined by the official religion to an obedience which deprives it of the power to think and examine for itself. Is it any wonder that this deprivation makes it the obvious prey of those Oriental superstitions which weaken the fibre of the nation long before the barbarian was knocking at the gate?

And this, I take it, is why, when the Christian faith begins to win acceptance, it is rapidly transformed from the simple doctrines we find in the New Testament, doctrines which clearly make of Jesus one figure, however mighty, in the long record of Hebrew prophets who, like Amos or Hosea or the second Isaiah, are seeking to make their creed a means of obtaining social justice for the humble man, into the complex theology which enables the Roman emperor to be a Christian and yet to maintain the elaborate hierarchy of Roman society, even to use the Christian creed to strengthen its hold. The intellectual of the early Church, like his predecessor in the pagan empire, presides over a mystery, and does not reveal a truth. Those whom he serves are not in quest of justice or of truth. They have lost that confidence which, in the sixth century before Christ, led their great predecessors to understand that as the veil is torn away from the face of nature, the common man can become, through knowledge, the master of his own destiny. There could not be a victory for the scientific interpretation of the universe without the overthrow of that vested interest in religion which, both in Greece and Rome, kept a small, privileged oligarchy in power. Progress in scientific knowledge meant progress in democratic institutions. Paganism resisted enlightenment for the masses lest its oligarchy should lose its power. When Christianity came, it enlarged the power of conscience, but its sources and its protection were alike an assurance that it would not enlarge the power of reason. In the result, it had relatively little influence on the realm of social constitution because, as it was shaped by Paul and his successors, it emphasized this life only as the vestibule to eternity, and put the chief importance of its dreams on the next world rather than upon this. Those who shaped its dogmas were thus, with but occasional exceptions, uninterested in the problem of giving the masses that map of the universe without which they cannot sail their ship into harbour. In a profound way, it was hardly until the period of the Reformation that the claim of reason to its dominion began to recover something of the passionate intensity it possessed in the Ionia of the sixth century or in that noble epitaph which Lucretius wrote upon the tomb of its hopes.

There is an enlargement of the power of conscience with the rise of Christianity; the recognition of the claims of reason has to wait for something like a thousand years before it receives proportionate acknowledgment. And within four centuries of the Reformation, when the revolution effected by Kepler and Descartes, Copernicus, Galileo, and Newton, has begun to make clear some, at least, of the results involved in the collapse of all orthodox creeds, the outstanding fact upon which we have to build is the knowledge that few modern men and women believe in the existence of a kingdom beyond this world in which an omnipotent deity judges men in the light of their behaviour upon earth. Four centuries of critical inquiry, historical, philosophic, scientific, anthropological, psychological, have had two overwhelming consequences. On the one hand, they have made it difficult for any person seriously concerned to accept, on rational grounds, the results of this critical inquiry, to accept the formulas by which any of the main orthodox religions promise salvation to man; on the other, they have made it equally difficult for the ordinary person to accept the view that a member of any particular Church is likely to be influenced in his daily conduct by the fact of that membership. No doubt there are millions of people to whom the truths of the supernatural faith they happen to hold are the most precious possession in life; but, equally, there are millions to whom such truths are wholly devoid of meaning. Christianity here, Mohammedanism there, Hinduism elsewhere may claim dominion over some special area in the world. But, even where this is so, that dominion does not mean the victory of justice and mercy and fraternity in the society it controls. There is bitter poverty in Iraq, which is predominantly Mohammedan, as there is bitter poverty in Spain, which is predominantly Roman Catholic, and as there is bitter poverty in the United Provinces of India, the religious texture of which is overwhelmingly Hindu. In each of these places, also, indifferently to their religious creed, the inhabitants are divided into a small number of wealthy persons with the power, born of their wealth, to overcome the main material problems of life, and a very large number of poor persons who either hover on the border line of failure, or are driven, by a complex of circumstances in which it is difficult to attribute personal fault to the overwhelming majority, over the edge of the abyss. As an intellectual issue, therefore, whatever religious faith may do for individual happiness, it is difficult not to conclude that it has no relevance to the collective problem of happiness by which our civilization is confronted.

The only working assumption, I suggest, upon which we can proceed is the simple, but important one that where the drive of some given society is towards an effort to make its material circumstances favourable to mass well-being, the inner life of its citizens will be shaped towards the realization of happiness. By this I do not mean for one moment that we shall all be assured of happiness when there is a decent house and a decent wage for every family, with free medical service and a wireless set in every home. I think it is hardly possible to deny that, were this to be the case, the increase in human happiness would be immeasurable; the number of those who find a full response to the cravings of their nature in the kind of poverty which attracted the Desert Fathers is relatively small; and the number of those who find fulfilment when, say, they tramp from factory to factory in search of the job which always eludes them, is, I think, still smaller. Nor does this exclude, for one moment, the fact that there are men and women who find fulfilment in that pursuit of the unworldly end which may drive them to poverty or exile or prison or even death.

I am concerned only to affirm that, as a working assumption for the people who live, not upon the heights, but in this work-aday world, adequate external circumstances are likely to mean adequate internal fulfilment. This is the humanism which, as I think, has a basis in the common principles of human nature all over the world, and transcends in its importance today, as it has transcended throughout human history, the appeal of any special religious creed which crusades for the renovation of man's nature. And it then follows from this assumption that the greater the degree in which external circumstances all over the world are made adequate, the greater will be the number of satisfied men and women. Good, on this view, is the satisfaction of demand on the largest possible scale; and a good society is one built upon an institutional basis which enables it perpetually to reach out to an ever increasing satisfaction of demand.

XII

Bolshevism and Capitalism

ALL this may seem elementary and even obvious; yet we are fighting the second World War in our own generation in response to the effort of the ruling classes to refuse acceptance of its consequences. And, in the years between those wars, especially in the years after the advent of Hitler to power, it was pretty clear to every serious observer that we moved by giant strides to a new Armageddon. We held conferences to organize disarmament; we held conferences to insist that international disputes must be settled by peaceful means; by the Pact of Paris, we outlawed war as an instrument of national policy with immense solemnity; and the economic experts met at Geneva to tell us, in a series of unanimous resolutions, how we could improve the world's standard of life. Year after year, the Assembly of the League of Nations provided a platform upon which eminent statesmen spoke to the world of the needs it faced. Year after year the conference of every religious denomination in the Christian world gave expression to their hope that the differences between nations would be settled without recourse to war. Probably at no time in the history of the world have the causes of war been examined with such care or in such detail; and I think it is true to say that at no time, also, was there less desire among the nations for martial glory, or a deeper appreciation of the ugly consequences of war. If, in 1914, girls threw roses to the troops as they marched to entrain, in the days around Munich, in 1938, there was not a cheer for war in any capital of Europe; and even the shameful surrender arranged at Munich hardly caused a sigh of pity for its victims, so great was the relief that conflict had been averted.

Yet war came inescapably, despite all this, a year later; and it exacted, month by month, its pitiless toll. In a sense, though its casualties were less than in the war of 1914–18, its cost was greater. For it involved in its path nations whose only relation to the dispute was the territorial accident of their strategic position, and because it bred hates which went far deeper than any produced by the earlier tragedy, it was marked by cruelties proportionate to those hates; nothing like the massacre of the Jews in Germany and Poland, or like the deliberate extermination of Lidice, would have occurred as even thinkable in the first World War. And it is important to realize that, in this second conflict, the Churches of the world were wholly without influence; their role was confined to that of praying for the victory of the particular nation in which they functioned. The Vatican, from time to time, explained that war is a terrible thing; but it made no impact on either rulers or ruled on either side save as a source of influence which both the United Nations and the Axis powers sought to mobilize on their behalf.

Nor has it been easy to trace any special influence in the intellectuals of any nation. Since propaganda has been a weapon of special importance in this war, a large number of them, in all the nations, have found a natural place as its instruments. But none of them has emerged to give to the war effort that special quality of purpose which has made some song or music, some poem or pamphlet, a source of inspiration to the fatigued soldiers or civilians in their grim movement to victory or disaster. I am not sure that there is not a sense in which it is true to say that, compared with the last war, the contribution of the intellectuals lacked a certain directness and spontaneity. For, first, the propaganda arm of government assumed the impersonality of an official technique; so that if the intellectual's propaganda had a quality of its own, it was likely to be displaced by material which conformed more fully to the departmental prescription. It is, no doubt, true that some half-dozen leaders among the statesmen of the world, above all, perhaps, Mr. Churchill in his first year as Prime Minister, President Roosevelt in his address to the Congress of January 6, 1941, and Marshal Stalin, in his proclamation to the Russian people on the recapture of Stalingrad, spoke words which the masses strained to hear, and, from lesser figures, there emerged now and then a phrase which lingered, like Mr. Henry Wallace's "century of the common man," and lingered gratefully, in public thought. But the size of the battle was too vast, the noise of its planes and guns too loud, for the voice of the intellectual to penetrate very far. What stood out most in the mind of the masses, was, even when unconsciously, the thing that Pericles said in the Funeral Speech at Athens: "freedom means happiness, and courage means freedom; do not trouble yourselves unduly about the dangers of war."

Certainly among the United Nations it cannot be said that anyone was "unduly troubled about the dangers of war." Whether it was the fighting men or the civilians, they exhibited a courage it would be insolent to praise. But, by the end of the fourth year of war, there was no one who could say with any assurance that their courage meant freedom, even in the days when the shape of victory began to define itself. That their courage would mean their freedom, and that in its attainment they would win the happiness implied in a life no longer shadowed by aggression, they were assured on every side. If promises can build a new world by their abundance, their happiness, after danger, was as certain as they could desire. Yet it was difficult not to remember the luxuriant rhetoric of the first World War and the empty years of cynical disillusions to which it was the prelude. Everyone could see that there would be one dazzlingly supreme moment when, all over the world, the blackout would be lifted, and the blaze of the lights which shone out once more would seem to portend the birth of new hope. But everyone, too, was almost afraid to look beyond that moment lest, as in 1918, the new hope should perish almost as it was born. If freedom means happiness, as Pericles said, are all the millions, men and women, who in the five continents have fought for freedom, having secured its safety, to have happiness, too? What changes were there in the distribution of effective power which offered a prospect of happiness different in its nature from the prospect upon which society entered when, on November 11, 1918, the armistice was signed and the conditions created in which, as their rulers told them in confident pride, the world had been made safe for democracy?

It is true that the significance of the Russian Revolution is unmistakable. For, with all its grave limitations—and they have been grave indeed—it has created in the masses of the Soviet Union the will to dedicate themselves to a great purpose beyond a purely personal end; and in the work of dedication they have found, amid the difficulties they have had to face, material improvement and spiritual elevation. This is the inner secret of all authority which has the power to effect a social renovation. It is, indeed, the source of the power religion has exercised over men in its moments of most intense creation. No one is now entitled to doubt that there is developing in the Soviet Union those qualities of mind and heart which gave to the Greek city-state at its best its capacity to raise the moral stature of its citizens. There is a pride in the common task, a discovery in the social purpose of the means whereby the individual can secure fulfilment. Out of all this slowly, perhaps painfully, too, there are being born before our eyes the characteristics of a great civilization.

What, I suggest, is outstandingly important in the Russian Revolution has been its revision of that attitude which, from the very dawn of recorded history, has looked with contempt upon manual labour, and regarded the masses who lived by its exercise as separated, in Xenophon's phrase, from the possibility of social and civic life. There is nothing in the Russian principle of that spirit which led to the downfall of France, and was put by Atticus in a phrase that might almost have been used by the rich collaborators of Pétain and Laval: "If the republic be lost, at least save our property." The contrast between the fear of the privileged classes in France that Paris might be bombarded, and the proud determination with which the Russians sacrificed the great dam on the Dnieper is too significant to be omitted. It is the contrast between a ruling class which identifies the hope of civilization with the perpetuation of its power on the terms of its past, and a whole people which has faith in its future. And that faith is the outcome of a great lesson learned from the unity of co-operation, a unity made all the more profound because it refuses to organize authority upon an antithesis between the worker by hand and the worker by brain. It is in the combination which has grasped the significance of this unity that the driving force of the Russian idea is to be found. It makes material advancement the outcome of this common effort, and it puts the whole spiritual and intellectual heritage of the race at the disposal of this combination. Thereby, it opens the career to the talents upon a scale that is, I think, genuinely new in the history of civilization; and it is in principle so organized that the emergence of talent is a factor in a social not less than an individual equation. This is a discovery which may well prove comparable in its importance with the effect upon mankind of the Christian claim that all men may be saved. It is, indeed, true in a sense to argue that the Russian principle cuts deeper than the Christian since it seeks salvation for the masses by fulfilment in this life, and, thereby, orders anew the actual world we know.

No doubt it is true of the Russian Revolution, as it has been true throughout the history of the Christian Churches, that it has offered opportunities to evil men of which they have taken large advantage. Any fundamental change which depends for its effect upon new human relations and institutions must run the risks inherent in the exercise of power. There is the constant temptation to confound the means with the end. There is the stifling of the voice of conscience which affects all men who hear the enchanting clamour of public applause. There is the danger of exacting by violence what could, were the effort patiently made, be won by the persuasion of consent. There is the risk of accepting as allies men who are less anxious to share the purpose sought than the authority which power confers; one can easily fail, especially in a critical period, to distinguish between the insincere supporter and the honourable opponent. Not least, there is the anxiety to achieve results that one can see oneself, which has so often sacrificed the individual to the organization, and mistaken a servile acceptance of some proposal for a genuine allegiance to its informing idea. And because the basic principles of the Russian experiment are new as practice, they tend to beget in those responsible for their application a passion for uniformity which threatens alike the uniqueness and the spontaneity of the men and women to whom they are applied. Yet, when all is said against the Russian Revolution that can be said, like the early Christian Church it impresses both the imagination and the conscience of its time in a way that gives a new and hopeful perspective to the history whose prospects it foreshadows.

It is important to note the historical significance of its central idea. We have so often been told that the principles of a socialist society are no more than the theoretical protest of the unsuccessful against a world which has denied them both the power and the glory, that it is almost impossible to exaggerate the vital significance of what the Russian Revolution has achieved. It has proved that the socialists were right who denied the universal and final validity of the acquisitive motive. It has shown that there is no inherent reason why progress should be the outcome of the exploitation of man by man. It has demonstrated how needless it is to assume that relations of production are creative only when their instruments are confided to private hands. No one who examines with any care the experience of the Russian experiment will be entitled to say again that the masses of a community do not contain an immense and perpetual reservoir of talent which the acquisitive society is unable either to discover or to utilize. No one, either, can honourably deny that the Soviet Union has proved beyond dispute that in a socialist society the use of leisure can be both dignified and creative. Nor does it appear from its experience that the permanent inequalities of capitalism can alone provide the savings which make possible the development of industries dependent upon the provision of capital goods. And it is a fact beyond dispute that the economic system of the Soviet Union has given to the ordinary worker the right to a say in the conditions under which he labours which he can only secure in a capitalist society either, as with a professional worker, by the possession of extraordinary talent, or, as in the worker whose task is within the confines of some well-defined routine, because he has behind him a strong trade union of whose policy the employer must take account. The Russian experiment, in a word, makes industry and agriculture something more than the cash-nexus between master and man. It transforms them, as socialists have always argued it would, into an avenue through which the worker passes to a deeper appreciation of all that citizenship implies. A system which, in its first generation, employs citizens and not "hands" has already found a way of making their personalities significant in the hours of toil which is rare under capitalism save where the worker is a man of exceptional significance in the process of production.

And these characteristics, it may be noted, have emerged in a time of quite exceptional strain, not merely in the Soviet Union itself, but over most of the civilized world. Anyone who compares the working of Bolshevik principles with those which apply in capitalist states must bear in mind two things. First, it is important that the international situation made the leaders of the Soviet Union—wisely as we now see—to industrialize at a pace which meant the deliberate subordination of the consumers' needs to those of the capital-goods industries, and, among these, to the industries relevant to the task of military defence; if it be said that the cost of this decision was tremendous, it is, I think, a sufficient answer that had this decision not been made, it is difficult to see any way in which Hitler could have been prevented from becoming certainly the master of Europe, and perhaps master of the world. And, second, it is important that throughout the years from 1917 until 1941 there was no capitalist society which was not anxious for the downfall of the Soviet Union, unwilling to build normal relations, either social or political with its people. The simplest test of this attitude is the outlook of Mr. Winston Churchill. The moment that the Soviet Union became strategically valuable to Great Britain, he was able to regard a partnership with it as necessary and desirable; "the bestial appetites and passions of Leninism" which he recorded in 1927, when Great Britain was not in danger, disappeared, as it were, overnight. Mr. Churchill came to see, between 1933 and 1939, that however "cancerous" might be the "Bolshevik growth," the performance upon it by Hitler of a surgical operation would be the end of Britain as a first-class power; it was the emotional sentiment of a great patriot, and not the reasoned conviction of a man who had penetrated to the heart of things, which led Mr. Churchill to change his view. But none of us must forget that emotional sentiments of a similar type had led Mr. Churchill, between 1917 and 1922, to do all in his power to secure the overthrow of the Bolshevik experiment precisely on account of those "bestial appetites and passions" against which, in 1927, he was still able to regard the Fascist principle as a safeguard. And, even in 1936, Mr. Churchill was displaying a zeal for the Spain of General Franco which it is difficult not to interpret as an enthusiasm for the traditional privileges of the aristocracy to which he belongs when those principles were called into question by the Spanish masses.

We have lost the faith by which the poor and the humble in our civilization accepted poverty and humility as their inevitable lot in life, in the belief that the ancient gods or some more modern dispensation would find them compensation in the next world for their hard fate in the present one. And it is the outstanding importance of the Russian idea that it is, above everything, a proclamation to the poor and the humble that the criteria by which they have measured their claims are devoid of rational validity. In essence, the Russian idea is nothing so much as a revival of that faith of the men of Ionia in the sixth century before Christ that men are saved by the chance of that abundance which comes from their mastery over nature. In that revival there is implicit a philosophy of life which makes men free of knowledge, without regard to class or race, and deprives the gods of their power to terrify the masses into acceptance of subordination. There is, in fact, nothing curious or unexpected in the long years of hatred the Soviet Union has experienced. It was the same fear that Epicurus and his followers encountered; and, in the last years of the Roman Republic, Cicero was using the kind of worldly wisdom with which our own generation has become so ironically acquainted to explain that it was no more than a fantastic dream to imagine that the poor could, as a class, emerge from their poverty and ignorance. And just as the Epicurean philosophy created a sense of dismay in the traditional rulers of Rome, because its appeal awakened in the masses a sense of excitement instead of their wonted torpor, created a prospect of hope instead of what, in a vivid phrase, that great pioneer in public health, Sir John Simon, called the "monotonous hunger for hope . . . which presses towards degradation of personal character and conduct,"[1] so the pioneers of the Soviet Union have created, almost everywhere, the same sense of dismay until the hour when their strength was sorely needed; and, even when that strength was given in generous measure, those who were advantaged by it remained uncertain of, not seldom unhappy about, its eventual outcome.

It is, of course, obvious that this mood which builds a partnership through which there run the threads of doubt and fear may as easily breed the fanaticism of hate as it may give rise to the affection of loyalty. Danger sharpens men's minds to an attitude of temporary receptiveness, but, when danger passes, it is always easier to abide by the ancient ways than to strike out on a new path the end of which is not known. Just as men as civilized as Marcus Aurelius, in one period, or Edmund Burke, in another, can, in the one case wearily, in the other with passionate anger, persecute the men of innovating ideas, so, in our own day, men with the power to lead, or in the place that invests them with authority, may prefer the old tradition to the new opportunity and fight with all their power of mind and

---

1 *English Sanitary Institutions* (ed. of 1897), p. 446.

heart to preserve it. There is no inherent reason why our civilization should, as it reaches the cross-roads, inevitably take the right direction; and this is especially the case in that difficult phase of its life when its renovation so largely depends upon those who have benefited from its ancient habits being able and willing to accept and apply a new way of life.

For at the point where, as with ourselves, the quest for a new philosophy of values is also a search for the instruments of political power, we are confronted with the extraordinarily difficult problem of whether those who can define the new philosophy can seriously influence, much less convince, the men who are to exercise the power. Men and women, no doubt are so constituted that, under the political systems of most, at least, of the United Nations, it becomes incumbent upon their leaders to define the ends for which their citizens are to risk their lives at least in general terms. It is the Four Freedoms; it is the century of the common man; it is relief from the shadow of aggressive attack; it is a world in which there is full employment for everyone; it is the due recognition of the rights of nations to security and independence; it is a society planned for abundance instead of one which is geared to the economics of restriction. *Tot consules quot sententiae;* the leaders on either side strive to outbid one another in the portrait of the splendid future which awaits on victory. Yet the wise man will remember that between promise and performance there is a gap not easily bridged. No leader of a nation at war dare reject a great principle which seizes the imagination of the multitude; but it is one thing to refuse rejection of a principle, and another, and very different thing, to give it the concrete reality of living and effective operation. "It is unnecessary," wrote Machiavelli in the *Prince* four hundred years ago, "for a Prince to have all the good qualities which I have enumerated. But it is very necessary to appear to have them . . . to appear merciful, humane, religious, upright, and to be so, but with a mind so framed that, should you require not to be so, you may have the ability and the knowledge how to change to the opposite."

Machiavelli, I venture to think, was writing of a world as living in our day as in his own. And his shrewd refusal to allow the power of the dream to conjure away the reality is a quality we should do well to emulate. For when, at long last, the enemy lays down his arms, the politics with which we shall be concerned will be concerned with the reality and not with the dream. "I fought," the Prime Minister can say, "to give you victory over your enemies; I made no pledge that I would lay my hand to the construction of a new social order." Sir John Anderson and Mr. Herbert Morrison may agree that they accepted many of the main principles of the Beveridge Report; but they can also insist that their acceptance was contingent on the state of the national finances when their legislative enactment had to be considered. "There is nothing," they may say, "we should so much wish for as the chance fully to implement its proposals; but, alas, given the condition of the Exchequer, he would be a reckless minister who thought that this was the suitable moment for action." Mr. R. A. Butler can insist that his White Paper displays a realization more full than any previous British Government has shown that the quality of a democracy depends upon the education of its citizens; yet it is not cynicism but, in the light of history, no more than a wise precaution to remember how little was left of the Fisher Act after the Geddes axe had hacked at its clauses. There is the vast problem of reconstructing our cities; and no one who examines the published plans for London and Southampton, to take two examples only, can doubt that their local authorities approach the task of reconstruction with an imaginative enthusiasm we have not seen since the great days when business men transformed the dream of Sir Christopher Wren into that abortive nightmare about which only Cobbett has written with adequate vigour. But that reconstruction depends upon decisions of the War Cabinet on matters like the Uthwatt Report, the future of the building trade, price-control in building materials, the authority to determine industrial location, which are postponed from month to month until it is not easy to evade the suspicion that vested interests are anxious to prevent any decisions being made until victory has taken from their making the vital perspective of urgency and disinterestedness.

This central idea of the Russian Revolution that we must, as a society, plan production for community consumption has taken a hold upon mass-opinion with something of the vigour of a new faith; with enough, at any rate, of that faith to make the Conservative Party's sub-committee on educational reconstruction warn us of the need to remind ourselves that this is a world of pain and sin, in which the larger hope, which the spectacle of Russian achievement may be permitted to arouse, becomes a threat to the security and order of a well-governed society, which means, no doubt, a society in which the masses are respectfully aware of their proper place.[1] And, in the United States, by far the richest country in the world today, one hundred thousand teachers in rural areas, thousands of whom earn less than six hundred dollars a year, left their jobs in the period from May to October, 1942; it is not remarkable to learn from men like Senator Thomas that enough men have been rejected by the American Army to supply fifteen divisions.[2] And anyone who examines the habits of Mr. Jesse Jones, the Secretary of Commerce in the Roosevelt administration, especially as these have been revealed in the course of his dispute with Vice-President Wallace, will be tempted to conclude that when Mr. Jones told the House Committee on Appropriations in February, 1943, that "we do not have anybody in our organization that has queer ideas," it is not wholly impossible that he included the central idea of the Russian Revolution among the "queer ideas" that he has banned. And among the "queer ideas" are, pretty clearly, for Mr. Jones, those on electric power with which the name of President Roosevelt is particularly associated in the United States; it is difficult, otherwise, to explain his refusal to carry out the President's instructions for a loan to be made

---

[1] Cf. my *Reflections on the Revolution of Our Time* (New York, 1943), p. 333f., where full quotations are given.

[2] *The Nation* (New York), July 10, 1943, p. 33.

to the Bonneville Power Authority to buy out the inadequately equipped but privately owned Puget Sound Power and Light Company in order to make fuller provision for the new war industries of the North-west.[1] Mr. Jones is, no doubt, as ardent in his desire to win the war as any of his colleagues in Mr. Roosevelt's cabinet; but it is legitimate, I think, to infer from the policies he is prepared to approve that the end for which he seeks victory must leave the world safe for those vested interests of big business of which he is the trusted representative.

It is no use our seeking to assume that the problems our civilization faces today are likely to be solved by the fact of victory. We cannot solve those problems without it; but, when it is accomplished, it is useless to pretend that it does more than provide the conditions under which they can be squarely faced with all the energies at our command. And as we approach the position where victory becomes a rational speculation, what begins to emerge as the most vital of all our problems is the need of a common faith by which to live. Western civilization had that common faith when the masses were prepared to accept the Christian promise of salvation as a means of compensating them for a poverty and suffering for which they could not be held directly responsible. But, with the erosion of any general faith in that promise, the kingdoms of this world seem, as they appeared to Saint Augustine, vast organizations of bandits in which the well-being of the many is systematically sacrificed to the advantage of the few. It is difficult to believe that such societies can endure unless the wealth at their disposal is sufficient to enable them to satisfy the wants of the masses. It is still more difficult to believe in their endurance when over against them is set the contrast of a society which, like the Soviet Union, has been able to pass beyond that acquisitive principle which still underlies all the main habits of the capitalist democracies. It is, indeed, more than probable that, at an early stage in the relationships of the United Nations, the contrast will become a challenge. For just as the inner life

1 See an illuminating article by Mr. I. F. Stone in the *Nation* of July 10, 1943.

of a society cannot continue where it is half-slave, half-free, so a commonwealth of nations is bound to be divided against itself when it is lacking that ultimate unity in diversity which is the real secret of peace. That is the only source of harmony in the life of states, the conviction in its members that they share in a purpose greater than themselves. But to have that conviction, they must not be oppressed by material cares, still less feel that it is by their oppression only that their neighbours have attained the freedom which security brings.

There is no way out in some vast embrace of the ascetic ideal. For, first, the number of those to whom asceticism presents itself as an ideal is certain to be small; and, second, a social philosophy that hopes to have functional significance must be one of which the principles seem rational and just to average men and women. When the Christian Church was able to impose its beliefs on the vast majority, it was able, also, to lend the support of its authority to the secular order of which, so to say, it was the partner. But its capacity to impose its beliefs lies everywhere in ruins about us; it lives, less by the conviction it evokes from citizens, than from the authority that is lent to it by the secular order; and it is evident from the experience both of Germany and of Russia that, if the secular order is overthrown, the religious organization it has used as one of its instruments is likely to be overthrown as well.

We thus confront the stark issue of finding a common faith in our civilization which accepts as finally ended the compulsive power of any ecclesiastical organization, with its claim to bestow salvation upon its votaries. No experiment upon which, in all his tragic destiny, man has embarked has faced so immense a problem. In essence, as the makers of the socialist philosophy have always seen, it seeks the acceptance of the argument that the elevation of the spirit of man can be achieved by a philosophy of value which defines the true and the good and the beautiful in terms which do not require for their authority the sanction of supernatural support. Of its power to inspire the extraordinary man, the philosopher like Epicurus, the poet like Lucretius or Shelley, the statesman like Jefferson or Lincoln or Lenin, there is ample evidence. But the power we need is, after all, one that maintains the faith in ordinary persons, and maintains it in them in ordinary times. Those humble men in Judea who laid the foundations of the Christian Church were sustained by a magic vision which reason, because it could not enter its temple, was powerless to destroy. The men who seek, through the ideals of the Russian Revolution, to revitalize the values of our civilization, submit their dream to tests of reason and of logic which, so far in history, have rarely maintained its splendour when its first rapture has died away.

XIII

The End and the Means

"THE vigour of civilised societies," Professor Whitehead has written,[1] "is preserved by the widespread sense that high aims are worth while. Vigorous societies harbour a certain extravagance of objectives, so that men wander beyond the safe provision of personal gratifications. All strong interests easily become impersonal, the love of a good job well done. There is a sense of harmony about such an accomplishment, the Peace brought by something worth while. Such personal gratification arises from aim beyond personality." In this sense I think the Soviet Union has discovered the secret of vigour, and, therein, the means to that common faith which binds men together in peace.

I know, of course, the case that can be made against this view. The common faith which binds men together in peace has involved the OGPU and the treason trials, the long list of men expelled from the party, or sent into exile, the government control of the written as well as of the spoken word. I am not more entitled, some critics will argue, to speak of this common faith born of the Russian Revolution than of a common faith built by Fascism in Italy or by Nazism in Germany. All of them lack that foundation in the free will of men that is essential to the building of a faith that will live. All of them depend upon the coercive power at the disposal of the governments which impose them; if Mussolini is overthrown, Fascist doctrine, as a faith, collapses like a pack of cards. So it will be with Nazism; and the liberal critic, especially if, like Élie Halévy, he sees an inherent contradiction between socialism and democracy,[2] will

1 A. N. Whitehead, *Adventures of Ideas* (1933), p. 371.

2 *L'Ère des tyrannies* (Paris, 1938), p. 213f.

make the same prediction about the future of the revolutionary idea in Russia. And he will emphasize particularly that there is no sign in the Soviet Union even of an approach to the fulfilment of Marx's prophecy that, with the advent of the classless society, the state will wither away.

I believe this argument to be wholly misconceived. But it is so widely and so generally held that it deserves, I think, a more careful examination than it has usually received either from those who accept it, on the one hand, or from those who reject it on the other. The attempt, in the first place, to identify the Bolshevist variant of Marxism with the doctrine of Mussolini or of Hitler seems to me monstrous error.[1] Mussolini was the typical Italian *condottiere* who used the crisis born of economic dislocation and frustrated nationalism to become the executioner of the democratic basis on which Italian capitalism was erected in the name, and with the assistance, of the forces of privilege in Italy—the House of Savoy, big business, the aristocracy, and the army. Without their support and, as soon as he was safely in power, that of the Vatican, a whiff of grapeshot would have disposed of his pretensions and those of the gangsters, like Grandi and Farinnacci, with whom he surrounded himself. He never had a doctrine worthy of the name of a philosophy or a faith; the bits and pieces from Sorel and Pareto, from Hegel and Gentile, which were accepted by his admirers as a *summa* would have seemed foolish if they had not been held together by monopolistic possession of the state-power. And, if on a vaster scale, the same is true of Hitlerism, though to the ingredients of the latter there must be added the claim of the Germans to be a chosen people, and the strength furnished it by its alliance with the historic tradition of Prussian militarism. In the understanding both of Fascism and of Nazism, it is essential to realize that they destroyed all workers' organizations, that they ruthlessly sacrificed the standard of life of the masses to preparation

---

1 Yet it attracts even so able a sociologist as Mr. Christopher Dawson. *Op. cit.*, p. 20, and, even more, my generous critic, Mr. George Orwell, *The Observer*, October 10, 1943.

for war, or for war itself; and that the sole compensation they had to offer in return for the slavery, both physical and mental, that they imposed, was the hope of a share in the loot of the conquests they hoped to make. The essence of both doctrines was the denial that the individual personality was of value in and for itself, and the consequential elevation of the state as an end in and through which by unquestioning obedience the masses found fulfilment. Both Fascism and Nazism were armed counter-revolution; and they lived, as they would die, only upon the basis of their ability to wage successful war. Both, therefore, decried the virtues of peace; for the leaders of both understood that peace would weaken the nationalist passion by arousing which they hoped to disguise the class war which remained implicit in the relations of production they preserved.

At bottom, this is to say, there is no real difference, except in the technological basis through which it is expressed, between Fascism and Hitlerism and tyrannies which are as old as history itself. That cannot be said of Bolshevism. Its origins go back, through the adaptation of Marxism to Russian conditions, to the slow rise of a protest by the working class against the Industrial Revolution and the emergence to power of a capitalist class which excluded the fourth estate from the hope of access to material well-being. The October Revolution sought to make that well-being the possession of the workers not less than of the men who were fortunate enough to own the instruments of production. It did not regard the state as an end beyond the individuals of whom it was composed. It denied the claim of those who by the ownership of property were able to make their demands effective to dominate the habits of society. It is, no doubt, true that Lenin and his followers assumed the inevitability of civil war. But that was not because they denied the validity of democratic government but because they were convinced that democracy can only assume a form that is real under the auspices of common ownership. Broadly speaking, their opponents looked upon liberty as the absence of interference with their disposition of power; the Bolshevists regarded freedom as the positive organization of opportunities for ordinary people to exercise a creative initiative. To achieve this end, they were driven to the idea of planned production for community consumption; and they required possession of the state-power if they were to accomplish this purpose. For, without the possession of that power, they would be unable to redefine the relations of production in society.

No one who analyses honestly the Soviet experiment can look upon its acceptance of a proletarian dictatorship as a permanent feature of the effort they were making. For, first of all, the sheer anarchy of the situation they inherited required a strong government if order was to be produced from the chaos they confronted.[1] And, in the second place, their effort to alter the relations of production in the Kerensky regime met not merely with opposition from the owners of property whose legal relations they sought to change, but also from all foreign powers which sought to influence them. The German attitude was revealed at Brest-Litovsk. Britain, France, Japan, the United States, even the Czech army, came to the aid of that series of sorry adventurers who sought to restore, if not the Tsar, at least the main social elements of the Tsarist regime. The adoption of proletarian dictatorship cannot, I think, be legitimately interpreted, as with the counter-revolutions of Italy and Germany, as a deliberate attempt to deny the spontaneity, and thus the significance, of human personality. On the contrary, anyone who honestly examines their attitude to education, to the position of women, to the rights of the backward peoples, to the problems involved in crime, to the place of science in the society they were seeking to build, and, not least, to the duties they laid upon members of the Communist Party, will find it difficult to avoid the conclusion that their objective was an advance in the welfare of all citizens, independently of class or creed or race.

For it is impossible, in any profound way, to examine the So-

[1] It is interesting to note how most historians of Rome praise Julius Cæsar and Augustus for ending the ugly anarchy of the Republic; their authority was "necessary." But when Lenin achieved the same result, his creation of order becomes at once "tyranny" or "the cancerous growth of Bolshevism."

viet experiment without seeing that its fundamental purpose was nothing less than the remaking of man. And the price of that remaking was, of necessity, not only a challenge to the past of Russia, and to the mass of Russians to whom, from 1917 onward, it was to be applied, but also to the rest of the world which built its relations of production on the acquisitive principle. Granted that challenge, there could not be democracy in the Soviet Union in the sense in which the democratic concept has meaning in Western civilization. For with ourselves the democratic concept is tied to a foundation which, for the overwhelming majority, makes a man significant and happy in terms of the volume of his possessions; and the politician who sought to loosen that tie would find himself at once in conflict with a mass of habits and laws and institutions all of which have been shaped by the insistence that wealth-getting is, in general, the source of significance and happiness. Wealth-getting, be it noted, for the individual on his own behalf; no conviction is more profound amongst us than the identity of common welfare with the aim of individual riches. It is this ultimate conviction that the Soviet Union denies; and if it is to prove its denial to the world, it has to alter all the habits and laws and institutions which have made it possible to impose that conviction on the great mass of mankind. It does not, therefore, seem to me remarkable that its denial has not yet proved compatible with an acceptance of the Western conception of democracy. If the Communist Party of the Soviet Union left the central principle of its faith to the chance decision of an electorate still in the phase where the denial of the socialist idea is the rule rather than the exception, that would be as remarkable as a willingness on the part of Western democracies to see without repining the access of socialist parties to the state-power. In fact, even the presence in office, in London or Paris, of Socialist ministers from whom no socialist legislation need be expected is sufficient to cause a panic on the stock exchanges of the world. And, in the creative days of the New Deal, when President Roosevelt was pushing legislation through Congress much or most of which was already a commonplace in the advanced European democracies, the alarm in Park Avenue, New York, seemed to suggest that he was the instrument of a hidden conspiracy the strings of which were pulled by Stalin in Moscow.

It is foolish, in fact, to expect that human behaviour can be fully adapted to the principles of a new faith in less than a generation, especially if those who are to be adapted are, in the process, to be urged to reject the faith on the ground that it is wholly irrational and contradicted by all experience. This is why the Soviet citizen is constrained to the acceptance of the fundamentals of his faith. We who are dismayed at this constraint ought, after all, to remember that the main reason why we are left the freedom to criticize the fundamentals of our own faith is that no one expects that freedom to criticize will become freedom to change; where this danger is even suspected upon the horizon, there emerge with startling rapidity the Mussolinis and the Hitlers and the Francos to put a term to that freedom. But the Soviet citizen enjoys what may perhaps be termed a democracy of a secondary order the import of which we must not minimize. He may not criticize Stalin or campaign against the Marxist philosophy, as the "economic royalist" in the United States can attack President Roosevelt and insist that the philosophy of the New Deal means ruin to America. But he can criticize his foreman or his manager; he can protest against the inefficiency of this factory or farm or even department of state. He can make suggestions which touch the pith of his daily life, and an anxiety on his part for self-improvement, whether in the work by which he earns his living or in some outside field of action, will not create for him the risk of being regarded as an agitator and so marked for unemployment, or as "getting above himself" and so likely to be unpopular with his fellows. The haunting fear of dismissal is not an omnipresent spectre in his home; and he need not fear that advancing years will mean the poverty that is born as he is forced out to make way for younger men. And the whole atmosphere in which he lives is pervaded by two factors the significance of which is among the first things to be noticed by a visitor to the Soviet Union. There is absent from it, first, that fantastic contrast between luxury and poverty which is so startling in the capitalist democracies; whatever the mistakes his rulers have made, at least they have not made the mistake of giving power to wealthy men just because they have wealth. The second factor is the recognition that work carries with it the status of dignity so long as it is useful and well-performed. Respect attaches not to the income earned but to the labour done; and the outcome of this factor in its operation is to open the way to the fulfilment which self-respect brings in its train which is a vital part of the secret of freedom.

The rulers of the Soviet Union are thus, in my own view, seeking to reshape the behaviour of man by a method of social organization which denies the claims made, in the Western world, on behalf of the acquisitive society. I do not for one moment argue that, in their effort at this reshaping, they have not often made immense blunders and committed fantastic cruelties; it is not less clear, as the trial of Yagoda made evident, that crime of a major kind has not been beyond the limits of the conduct their faith permitted them. I accept the ugliness of all these things; and I do not even attempt to excuse them. But those who set out to judge their import must see them in their historical proportion. Those who accept the Christian faith do not regard the stains upon its record as the disproof of its insight. Yet the persecutions, the simony, the nepotism, of the Churches have lasted down to our own day. Most Presbyterians today regret the burning of Servetus by Calvin; but they do not infer from that tragedy that Calvin's theology is erroneous. Few Roman Catholics would today defend the barbarities of the Inquisition; but they would deny that these barbarities disprove the validity of the Roman claim. The fact we have got to recognize is that any belief passionately held will seek to obtain power; and, if it does obtain it, it will fight with all its strength not merely to maintain the power it has won, but, if it can, to extend the area of its authority. That is true of a nation or a

Church or a state; and where the possession of a belief gives birth to controversy, it is only where its consequences are deemed unimportant that men are prepared to abide by the results of reason and peaceful discussion. If men could kill one another over minutiæ of theological difference which now hardly arouse even the interest of scholars, it is not really remarkable that, in barely a quarter of a century, the divisions between men over the validity of the Russian Revolution should still create fury on either side. And where there is fury, there men take up arms lest the cause of their opponents should prevail. In these conditions, the stage where government by the voluntary consent of the governed is possible has clearly not yet arrived.

If we are to understand the passion which a new faith arouses, we must set ourselves at some distance from the disputes in which we are ourselves involved. For then we have the chance of gaining a perspective which gives proportion to our judgment, of seeing the immediate dispute with something of the detachment and disinterestedness which are the conditions of wisdom. Nearly sixty years have passed since William Morris, in one of his socialist lectures, spoke of the coming breakdown of our society with that intensity of insight and imagination that the poet's vision compels. "Consider," he wrote,[1] "what a society founded on robbery means: how the meanest and most miserable vices flourish under it. I have said that our present system compelled us into cowardice, and therefore injustice. Is not that the natural consequence of a society wherein each who would thrive must do so at his neighbour's expense; must live in short by stealing? Under such conditions, there is nothing stable; for look you, it does not avail us that we have good capacities, that we are industrious, deft with our hands or our brains, well-developed human beings, all that is no use to us unless others are worse than we are; unless we can conquer them, they will conquer us, and in spite of our good qualities we shall be condemned to be their slaves, and thereby the greater part of our

---

1 May Morris, ed., *William Morris, Artist, Writer, Socialist* (Oxford, 1936), Vol. II, p. 432.

good qualities be wasted and lost. So that we live in daily terror lest we should lose, some of us our domination over others, some of us our leisure, some of us our decent livelihood; and that fear forces us, I say, to deal hardly with our fellow-men lest they should rise above us and take our places."

It is, as I have said, nearly sixty years since Morris used those words; it was in the year after he had begun to edit the *Commonweal* and had appeared in court, before Mr. Justice Saunders, after the free speech demonstration in Dod Street, Limehouse, of which old men still speak with pride. One can still, I think, catch the quiver of eager passion in his lecture even though he was well aware that the social order he was condemning was deep-rooted and strong. Ought not that eager passion to make us realize how far more intensely the faith would count with men who are not speaking of a future that they deem to lie ahead but of a present that they are safeguarding with their lives? It is not the language of exaggeration that Morris is speaking, but of sober realism. For we have seen this mood not only in the nations swept, in the inter-war years, by revolution and by counter-revolution. We have seen it in Britain in the days of the general strike, on February 6, 1934, in Paris, in Herrin and Paterson and Gastonia, in the United States. We must not forget that when Franco turned Spain into one vast prison-house, the Vatican accorded its support to the jailer of the Spanish people; and the history of Mexico since President Calles showed the Church of Rome in alliance with the oil magnates of Britain and America to maintain their power even at the price of mass poverty and peonage. That "daily terror that we should lose our dominion over others" describes not some sudden or sporadic state of siege but an attitude of mind which socialism, as a principle of action which, in Russia, possesses the state-power, is concerned decisively to destroy.

Historically, of course, there is grim reason to suppose that a civilization which collapses, as our own is collapsing, in war and revolution, will not easily attain the inner harmony of peace. We do not need to suppose, with historians even so eminent as

Rostovtzeff, that the decline of the ancient world was the outcome of an effort to spread its culture from an aristocratic *élite* to the masses; it is not, I think, fanciful to attribute that gloomy conclusion to the natural pessimism of a great scholar of the Tsarist regime who watches with dismay the rise of the third estate to power. All of us are tempted to suppose that the wisdom of the class we represent assures the grand climax of all civilized history; no one, for example, can read the second of Macaulay's famous speeches on the great Reform Bill [1] without the sense that there is a real truth in Bagehot's remark that he regarded "English history as a process leading up to the debates in which he had taken part"; [2] and few things are more remarkable than the complete confidence with which Barnave assumed that, with the triumph of the French *bourgeoisie* in the Revolution of 1789, history had reached the final boundaries of its possible development,[3] unless it is the simplicity with which an eminent American manufacturer assumed that his success in business was the direct outcome of God's will.[4]

In a world such as ours, in which the principles which underlie the organization of Western democracy are in an antithesis almost direct with those which underlie the democracy of the Soviet Union, it is far from easy to assume that victory alone will serve to provide a basis for their permanent reconciliation. It is suggestive that in Britain the alliance between the Conservative Party and the Labour Party is maintained by the prudent postponement of any discussion of the living issues upon which the people must decide when victory is won, rather than by the discovery of common ground which enables them now to find common assumptions. That is important because there is no sense in which the Labour Party can be regarded as a revolutionary party; it is an extension of the social radicalism of the Lloyd George period into a wider field of action. Its roots are still in that Fabian philosophy which assumes the primacy of reason

1 *Selected Speeches* (Oxford, 1935), p. 20f.
2 Quoted by Mr. G. M. Young in the edition cited, p. xii.
3 H. J. Laski, *The Rise of Liberalism* (New York, 1936), p. 267f.
4 Herbert Harris, *American Labor* (1939), p. 127.

in politics, and that despite the experience of the European continent in the inter-war years. It accepts, therefore, as an article of faith the willingness of its opponents to abide by the results of the democratic method, and looks to the piecemeal transformation of capitalist society in Britain to a socialist society. Whether it has seriously measured the position it will occupy at the end of the war, first in the light of 1931 and its grave implications, and, second, in the light of the burdens that even victory will put upon Great Britain, it is not easy to determine. The most natural conclusion to which one is led is that the outlook of British Labour is built, not upon any coherent philosophy, but upon a pragmatic approach which insists upon dealing with each issue as it arises; and this looks to the critical observer less like a truth than that historic British policy of "muddling through," the success of which, in the past, was due less to its inherent logical merit than to the immense economic advantages which Britain possessed, as against all nations save the United States, until the outbreak of war.[1] And it is not easy to see that, when this war is over, this chance of success is available for the simple reason that, in large part, at any rate, the economic advantages will have disappeared. Britain, so to say, will be back where it was at the end of the Napoleonic wars without the economic primacy it then possessed and without the self-assurance that was born of that economic primacy.

In such circumstances, it is hard to see that the habit without philosophy which characterizes an acquisitive society will offer the unity of outlook upon which social peace depends. If Mr. Churchill has his way, it is only when the war is won that the masses will be told the programme to which their assent is sought; and the character of that programme is to be determined by what it is thought the "nation" can afford at that time. But as soon as we begin to analyse the concept of the "nation" it becomes pretty clear that it is a body of voters which either decides to continue the Coalition Government over which Mr. Churchill presides, in which case the Labour Party becomes a kind of

[1] Cf. my *Marx and Today* (Fabian Society, 1943), *passim*.

permanent left wing of the Conservative Party, or the Coalition Government is broken, and the Labour Party appeals to the electorate on a socialist programme. In the first case, the main principle of a continuing coalition is the acceptance, in general outline, of the traditional character of British society, of a structure, that is, built upon the acceptance of the acquisitive principle. In the second, the Labour Party is bound to move towards a genuine philosophy which rejects the acquisitive principle. In the first case, it is at least unlikely that the Labour Party will be able to retain the genuine socialist elements among its members; and the rift which will then emerge in its ranks is likely to condemn it to the fate of the Liberal Party after 1918. What would then become important would be the evolution of a socialist faith, organized separately from the Labour voters who supported the idea of a continued national government; and the pace of that evolution would depend upon the character of the measures for which the reconstituted national government made itself responsible. And if we assume, as we are, I think, entitled to do, that the effective basis of such a government depended upon Conservative support, it seems to me reasonable to argue that the drift of its critics to a fully socialist outlook would be likely to be more rapid than present circumstances enable us to imagine.

That is still more likely to be the case if the Coalition Government ends with the defeat of Hitlerism. For, in that event, a Labour Party which had resumed a genuine independence would be bound to seek electoral support by proving the reality of its socialist principles. That proof, in my own view, would not be available upon the domestic plane alone. In the aftermath of victory, it is becoming obvious that two great faiths stand out in contrast to one another. The United States stands firmly by the view that the less there is of a planned society the greater the opportunity the individual is left for creative effort; and the Soviet Union, no less firmly, rejects that notion on the ground that, sooner or later, it is bound to create the conditions out of which a third world war will come. I am confident that a British

Government in which Conservative influence is predominant will incline to the American view; and, equally, I am confident that the attitude of the Soviet Union is more likely to prove right. For, with the end of the war, the United States will possess a capacity for production in excess of anything that any nation has known in history. To use it will involve one of three possibilities. It may retain its present relations of production; in that case, it must either win markets it can profitably exploit all over the world, or it will face unemployment on a scale even greater than in the great depression. The first alternative involves it in a massive economic imperialism; the second, I suggest, on all experience, not least the implications of American experience, will see the end of democratic life in the United States. For it is now beyond all question that mass unemployment and democracy in politics are contradictory principles. And if America embarks on economic imperialism, however unconsciously, granted the power at its disposal, it is difficult to see how the British Empire, which lives by exports, can retain its power without the kind of reduction in its standard of life which would be fatal to its traditional habits and organization.

There is, of course, the third possibility. The United States may have the wisdom to recognize two things. It may come to see, first, that the more fully it assists the nations of Europe and Asia to recover from the miseries of war, the more effective, in the long run, will be the prosperity to which it gains access; and it may realize that one of the profoundest economic mistakes in its history was when, in the inter-war years, it adopted a policy of high tariffs and barriers upon the free entrance of immigrants from Europe. It is not easy to see that its leaders will be likely to take this long-term view. American commercial interests have rarely been impressed by the emphasis of the economists upon the grave danger of high tariffs for the world; even under the auspices of the New Deal the diminution of the barriers against the freest possible international trade had been relatively small; and there is little evidence that American trade-unionism, the chief opponent of free immigration, has changed its view since

1939. No one, indeed, who examines with any care, not the utterances of unorganized intellectuals, but the policies of those who shape the predominant interests of the United States today, will be tempted into an optimistic mood. The National Association of Manufacturers, the Chambers of Commerce, the American Legion stand pretty firmly by that individualism which, after 1919, led through the Harding-Coolidge-Hoover epoch, into the great depression. The growth of feeling against the Negro, as shown in the race riots of Detroit, leaves the governors of the states involved bankrupt of any suggestion; Governor Sparks of Alabama, for example, attributed the evil to "outside influences," and seemed to imagine that the problem was solved by noting that "the two races are part of the economy of the South," with the obvious inference that their relation in that economy must be regarded as permanent.[1]

And it must be remembered that the relations of the American state—which is not the same thing as the American people—to European reconstruction raise psychological problems of power which it would be foolish to underestimate. All of us can see that America will throw all its weight into victory over the Axis. But victory for what and victory for whom? The Italians can see today, and the Germans will see tomorrow, how grimly they have been misled about the purposes of Mussolini and Hitler. But will they also see that they were misled by the propaganda which warned them not to believe the "Four Freedoms" were genuine if, in fact, nothing is done to make them genuine? Is there not implicit in Anglo-American policy in North Africa, perhaps, also, in that policy in Italy, as a prelude to its Italian expression, a warning to the masses that free institutions and economic justice for Europe are less important than such a shaping of the victory as will leave Babbitt and those upon whom he depends safe in the possession of their privileges? Enduring peace, on all the historic experience of capitalist democracy, is not logically inherent in its principles. For we must never forget that, in 1939, no people wanted war, and yet war came. It

---

[1] *The New Republic,* July 12, 1943, p. 38.

is, of course, a delusion to imagine that the coming of war was due, either in Italy or Germany, to the influence of "one evil man"; the real issue is the much more complicated one of the causes which led each of these nations, in the light of their history, to permit those "evil men" to obtain that influence over them. And that issue, in its turn, must be linked to the causes which led the governments of Britain and the United States, between the wars, to patronize those "evil men" and to listen, without embarrassment, to the eulogies heaped upon them by British and American citizens who lived in that "daily terror" of the masses of which William Morris spoke.

XIV

The Price of Freedom

"IN THE struggle which was necessary," wrote Thomas Jefferson of the French Revolution,[1] "many guilty persons fell without the forms of trial, and with them some innocent. These I deplore as much as anybody, and shall deplore some of them to the day of my death. But I deplore them as I should have done had they fallen in battle. It was necessary to use the arm of the people. . . . The liberty of the whole earth was dependent on the issue of the contest, and was ever such a prize won with so little innocent blood? My own affections have been deeply wounded by some of the martyrs to this cause, but rather than it should have failed, I would have seen half the earth desolated; were there but an Adam and Eve left in every country, and left free, it would be better than as it now is." It is a hard saying. Yet it is true of an acquisitive society, as it was true of the Europe of Jefferson's day that, because power is so overwhelmingly the expression of wealth, "every man must be either pike or gudgeon, hammer or anvil." [2]

The note that Jefferson strikes in the passage I have quoted from his observation upon the French Revolution is one that excites horror in most comfortable minds, and even in many that would claim a progressive outlook. Yet it is immensely important for us to remember that, all through the ages, the masses of mankind have lived very near the edge of disaster. It is hardly less important constantly to remind ourselves that most of the long-term sources of pleasure, the exercise of intellectual curiosity, the enjoyment of the æsthetic pleasure which comes from great poetry or great music or great literature, the planning of a

---

1 *Democracy: Selections from the Writings of Thomas Jefferson* (London, 1939), p. 32. The passage is from a letter of Jefferson's to Short, written in 1793.

2 *Ibid.*, p. 261 (Letter to C. Hammond, 1821).

career in politics, the decision to travel, have all of them been resources confined, as a means of satisfaction, to the few. And, for the most part, both in time and space, the authority of the state has been used to safeguard that confinement of resources and not to enlarge them. Even when Christianity achieved its association with imperial power, it did not operate to secure enlargement despite its origin as doctrine propounded by poor and humble men. That was in part due to the emphasis it laid, in its early years, upon the proximity of the Second Coming, and, in part, to the constancy of its faith in values not of this world. So that when the Roman Empire accepted it as the official religion, it had already undergone a subtle adaptation to the needs of the Empire which effected it, like the pagan creeds it supplanted, to the historic ways of earthly power. So that like Judaism, in its early phases, and the religion of the Greek city-state, the Christian Church became, over the centuries, a reinforcement of the very class divisions in society against which, so far as they could dare, its founders had passionately protested.

In all ages when the means of material well-being have been expanding there is an emergence of that atmosphere of hope which permits men to organize their relationships in terms of persuasion. Hope acts as a factor of unification; it enables men to see what they hold in common and this reduces in the proportion that it is widespread the need for force as the basis of authority. But the expansion of which the economic systems we have known have so far been capable have never been either continuous or intense enough to make the power of hope sufficiently pervasive to make consent rather than coercion the permanent thread with which the pattern of our lives is woven. It is, no doubt, true that during at any rate something like the last three or four centuries the level of response to demand, the power to overcome disaster and make life secure, in other words both the standard of life and the rule of law, have been more adequate than at any previous time. Not least, the pace at which, within this period, man has become the master of nature's secrets, and so brought his fate in increasing measure within his own control, is revolutionary compared with the changeless centuries between say Athens in the fifth century before Christ and the repudiation of the papal claims two thousand years later. And, in particular, the geographical discoveries, especially of America, set the old world in a perspective which had also revolutionary import.

For while it would be a gross exaggeration to say that America started, after its discovery by Europe, with a clean slate, it offered opportunities, from some such period as Franklin's growth to manhood, both to the indigenous American and the European immigrant, as he could not dream of attaining in the old world unless he was one of a very small and privileged class. One has only to try to measure the impact of the American ferment on France and Ireland, on Germany and on Italy, to recognize that it exacted in a hundred ways new standards of opportunity, new levels of treatment for the citizen by the state-power, which mark an epoch in the power of personality to secure fulfilment. The promise of American life, at least from the achievement of independence to the great depression of 1929, seemed to give to democratic institutions a new status amongst mankind. Certainly it is not excessive to say that in the century and a half this period covers any political system which denied the ultimate validity of the democratic hypothesis was felt to be, and, indeed in large part actually was, upon the defensive.

It would be an historical error of judgment to argue that the promise of American life was always a dream rather than a reality. But it is not, I suggest, an historical error to insist that the immense drama of the unfolding continent, with its immense resources and its power to absorb what seemed an endless stream of immigrants, its sudden creation of a literature which became, as at a bound, part of the mainstream of civilized thought, its capacity to breed statesmen who strode, like Jefferson and Lincoln, into the White House with a fitness which did not fear, nor need to fear, comparison, with any ruler born of the historic traditions of Europe—it is not, I suggest, an error to insist that the sheer splendour of the drama, the scale upon which it was mounted, concealed from the spectator that it was, for all its excitement, still no more than a new version of a play as old as the history of man. For from Shays's rebellion onward, through the fight between Federalist and Republican, in Jackson's conflict with Nicholas Biddle and his bank, in the four years of that grim mass-fratricide which Charles Beard has so rightly called the second American Revolution, then in that ugly period of corruption and squalor when the Goulds and the Vanderbilts, the Rockefellers and the Morgans, set out to write their commentary on the Gettysburg speech, we see the outline of the old acquisitive pattern being woven once more. There is protest against it from the earlier time, Populism, the Knights of Labour, the Progressive Movement; and some of the protests, like the insight of John Taylor of Caroline, or the angry ardour of Daniel De Leon, have a prophetic quality about them.

Yet, on the whole, it is true to say that until panic ushered in the great depression on that fantastic October 29, 1929, there were few Americans, and perhaps even fewer Europeans, who did not think that the United States had a special destiny reserved for it, different from the destiny of the old world. In a sense, the United States had taken the war of 1914 in its stride; and its aftermath had been ten years of boom conditions which concealed from most the fate that was waiting to prove that they who sow the wind must reap the whirlwind also. The years of the New Deal made it evident that the mental climate of America was not in essence different from that of any other acquisitive society. Its resources being greater, naturally enough, its foundations were stronger also; and it was therefore able to resist the pressure of social conflict with greater ease and for a longer period. But in the years between the entrance of President Roosevelt into the White House, and the Japanese aggression at Pearl Harbor, it is the general effect of massive inquiry into social and economic conditions in the United States that America, in the phrase of Mr. Archibald MacLeish, "was promises," but promises to millions who did not dare to build on their fulfilment. A generous, sprawling, kindly, hospitable civilization, deeply interested in freedom for the Indian and the Chinese, the Englishman and the Czechoslovak, unable to endure the thought of a Hitler-dominated Paris; but far less interested, with all its philanthropy, in freedom for the share-cropper in Arkansas, or the operative in the cotton mills of Gastonia, or the Negro in the Jim Crow car in Memphis or Atlanta, and certain that freedom was a gift Americans give instead of grasping the vital truth that freedom must always be taken and can never be a gift, especially never a gift to one's own fellow citizens. Nor, despite the great inheritance of magnanimity that is America's, did it seem to confront the issue set by Lenin in the Russian Revolution with that power of vital response to the challenge of a great experiment which Jefferson displayed in the face of the test that 1793 set to the generation upon which he impressed his own wise sense of historic proportion.

When perhaps about A.D. 50, in that accent of the Eastern Mediterranean which brought a smile to the faces of his Athenian audience, Paul stood on a rock below where the Acropolis towers with the Parthenon as its crown, pleading with his listeners to adopt a new way of life and telling them of the great revelation that had come to him who, such a little time before, had been amongst the most zealous persecutors of the new faith, the Athenians dispersed in laughter as they heard the ardour with which he spoke to them of principles which they knew were in plain contradiction to the historic truths of their own ancient faith. Yet it was the creed of Paul which before long had triumphed; and the pagan deities in whose honour the Parthenon had been built were replaced by an altar before which the men of Athens prayed to the God whom Paul had vainly besought them to accept.

It does not seem impossible that this may be the history, also, of that acquisitive society which now seems so strong and so impenetrable to that idea of mutual aid which the dreamers and the visionaries set over against it. For the acquisitive society, if it is to endure, must show its power not only to give men peace, but also to have the right to hope; and these it cannot achieve if the wealth that it produces still leaves the masses poor and still breeds the kind of crisis from which there is no outlet but war. It is not, of course, impossible that the democratic epoch in the history of Western civilization will prove, in fact, like slavery and feudalism, no more than a passing phase in its evolution, and that the power behind the capitalist principle will prove far stronger than any challenge the Russian Revolution can organize. No one who is aware of what men will do in the service of some system of ownership in which they passionately believe can doubt for a moment that the devotees of what is, in fact, essentially a religion of privilege will fight as hard as they can on its behalf. The English civil wars of the seventeenth century were an offering on the altar of a social system which had already crumbled into pieces when Charles I raised his standard at Nottingham; already, in 1601, Thomas Wilson estimated that the economic power of the gentry was some three times that of peerage and Church combined, even when the income of the wealthier yeomanry was added.[1] The fact that a cause is lost does not mean that men will not take the field on its behalf, as the tragic magnanimity of Lee makes clear; for only fantastic blunders on the part of the North could have lost it the Civil War.

And the religion of inequality cannot wisely be reckoned in any sense yet a lost cause. Outside the Soviet Union, its representatives are still the masters of the state-power in all the most powerful nations. Even if we agree that its prestige will be gravely weakened by the overthrow of the Axis powers, and that there is no country in which it does not now have to meet with a scepticism and disillusion not unlike the temper encountered by paganism in the last centuries of the Roman Empire, that attitude may well be the prelude less to its decay and dissolution than to a bitter epoch of creed wars, in which men fight for political and economic, instead of for religious principles. After all, it was for one social order rather than another that the wars

---

[1] Thomas Wilson, *The State of England A.D. 1600* (Camden Society, 1936), ed. F. J. Fisher.

of religion were waged in sixteenth-century France; as Mr. Trevor-Roper has well, if grimly remarked,[1] "the more we analyse the 'Wars of Religion,' the less of religion, properly so-called, do we find in them." What is true of the wars between Catholic and Huguenot in France is equally true of the battle between Anglican and Puritan in the England of the seventeenth century. The protagonists on both sides understood fully that the subject matter of their disputes, whatever the battle cries they used, was for the power to organize social behaviour in one way rather than another way. And this is not less true of the controversies of our own day. Nazi and Fascist seek to use German and Italian nationalism on behalf of privilege in Germany and Italy; and the masses in both countries are used as weapons in a conflict in which they have no real interest that is hostile to the interest of the masses in the United Nations. Nor is this less true of the use by the combined power of Japanese militarism and big business of the common people of Japan as the instrument through which it searches to dominate the Eastern world, it may well be, as the Tanaka memorandum forecasted, in prelude to a universal mastery.

The victory of the United Nations seems now to be a thing upon which we can count, though we are far from knowing yet the price we shall have to pay for its achievement. But when the victory is complete, that still leaves its meaning to be determined. It is not, let us be clear, a victory over the acquisitive society; only of the Soviet Union can we say with any assurance that this will be the case. It is, no doubt, wholly true that the defeat of the Axis powers is the essential prelude to the general transformation of the acquisitive society into socialist democracy. But what follows on that prelude is still an unwritten act in world history about the nature of which we have taken no decisions. It is not even certain, when the prelude is complete, that we shall be in a position to take decisions about its nature by agreement. There is a vast philosophic gulf, to take the most obvious example, between the picture of the future in the minds

[1] H. R. Trevor-Roper, *Archbishop Laud* (London, 1940), p. 3.

of the Council of People's Commissars in Moscow and the picture in the minds of the Polish Provisional Government in London. It is not yet clear that the kind of world envisaged after victory by Mr. Churchill is the kind of world likely to appeal to Marshal Stalin; such evidence as we have suggests that it is at least possible that they think on different lines. Each has praised with enthusiasm the effort of the other leader's people to fight the war to a victorious conclusion; but each has been careful, at least so far as public commitment is concerned, to paint the use to which victory, when it comes, will be put in terms so general that they involve no general principles of settlement beyond the common right to impose an unconditional surrender upon our enemies. But that still leaves quite undetermined the ends for which the unconditional surrender will be used. And if this difficulty applies to the relations between Marshal Stalin and Mr. Churchill, the latter of whom can at least be reasonably confident that he will secure the consent of Parliament to whatever conditions of peace he may propose, it is likely to be far more true of President Roosevelt, who does not know that he will, after November 1944, be still in the White House, or that, if he is, the Congress of the United States will be more amenable to his advice than its predecessor was to the treaty negotiated by President Wilson in 1919. And Mr. Roosevelt cannot, like Cromwell, send a Colonel Pride and a platoon of Democrats to rid him of a Congress which is anxious to have the final American word.

XV

The Great Cause

AN ACQUISITIVE society which has a faith by which to live can maintain the pursuit of a purpose which binds it together. Anyone who examines the colonizing experiments of the sixteenth and seventeenth centuries can see how the mixture of an advancement of the true religion and the achievement of at least the hope of profit can make men in Spain and Portugal, France and England and Holland mysteriously conscious that they share in a great destiny in which they find fulfilment. Whether it be the statesman like Francis Walsingham, the sailor like Drake, the parish priest who is half-geographer like Hakluyt, the adventurer like Raleigh, the business organizer like Sir Thomas Smythe, or the mystic poet like John Donne, there is a sense in all of them of a great conviction beyond themselves in which they live and move and have their being.[1] They are part of a great society in which, whatever its defects and weaknesses, the power to hold a great conviction which is more than the selfish desire for personal and material satisfaction gives vitality and creativeness. By this capacity for conviction I do not mean that conventional acceptance of some outlook, or even the acceptance of the ritual of its behaviour, in the way that leads a man into, say, the priesthood of the Church of England because there is a well-endowed living in the gift of the family which he can hope, after ordination, to fill. I mean an outlook chosen on grounds which go deeper than the satisfaction of one's self, that is capable of evoking sacrifice and the willingness to risk danger, and even death, on its behalf. All of us have known or read of men who have had this sense of conviction. It breeds in those

[1] Cf. L. B. Wright, *Religion and Empire* (Chapel Hill, 1943) for a brilliant and amusing account of the part played by the Church in empire-making in Tudor and early Stuart times.

who possess it the passion for adventure, that eagerness for novelty, that dissatisfaction with the standardized routine, which is the dynamic of all civilized living.

Historically, all great causes have had the power to evoke this temper, even causes in which we are now certain that the end was a mistaken one. But it is not, I think, excessive to say that no cause has ever evoked it either so widely or so deeply as the cause of freedom. It is when men and women feel that their cause is truly freedom that they have the fullest power to rise above whatever in themselves or their environment is mean or narrow or petty. That is why, in these grave years through which we are living, all of us have seen men and women whom before we thought were ordinary people capable of some act or idea which lifted them, if only for a brief space of time, to heroic stature; and it is upon that capacity that Mr. Churchill was able to build in those grim months of the Battle of Britain when, week by week, the chance of national survival seemed ever more completely a miracle of history. A society has faith when it is able to evoke this temper in its citizens, to have the consciousness that all the time some of them follow the dream that takes them beyond themselves, and that, in the supreme hour, the dream becomes possessed of the whole social consciousness.

It is my argument that, for the purpose of normal living, the acquisitive society that we know has no longer the capacity to evoke faith of this kind or quality. That is why, before the outbreak of war, its predominant expression in literature was that of satire; for it is when a society is seeking to preserve a system that has in fact gone beyond the power of renovation that satire becomes the most natural expression of its art. Poetry, fiction, criticism, painting, music, philosophy, in all of these it is above all the satirical temper which gives them their prevailing note. Satire is the refuge of the artist or the thinker who cannot pass beyond the boundaries of disillusion into the realm of positive faith. He must gibe or mock or lash in an indignant fury, because he cannot find in his time the right to the conviction he can justify to himself. We see this mood in the age of Lucian and of Juvenal. We see it in the savage irony of Byron after the tragic issue of the French Revolution or in that bitter mockery in which Heine strives to conceal the depth of his yearning for a faith he is entitled to hold. The satirist is the artist who cannot find inner peace because he cannot accept the values which the society of his time seeks to impose upon him, so that he rises in fury against them as a denial of the harmony which permits creativeness.

He may, of course, pass beyond satire, like Shelley, into the realms of an impalpable beauty; though the famous last lines of the great chorus in *Hellas,* like the inner melancholy which pervades the whole of *Adonais,* and the sonnet which he wrote in 1818 in which he warns us not "to lift the painted veil which those who live call life," or, again, the voice which, in the last year of his life, bids him die if he would "be with that which thou dost seek," and in the broken pathos of the poem, again of 1822, "when the lamp is shattered," all go to make it clear that Shelley could not dwell for long within those realms in the age of Sidmouth and Castlereagh and Eldon. Where, in fact, in an age in which the artist's natural weapon is satire because its values are repellent to any man of creative gifts, he can find contentment only when, like Coleridge, he has drugged himself beyond the capacity of coherent thought, and is reduced to flashes of inspiration, or, like Wordsworth, accepts an authority outside this world, whether he calls it Nature or God, upon which he can lean to secure relief from the torment of the contrast between actual and ideal. That is why the facile optimism of Emerson left Hawthorne and Melville bewildered and dismayed; [1] for, with a deeper insight than his, they saw that the summer he saluted with such rapture was the prelude to a stark winter of which, already, they felt the first chill. And that is why, also, I believe, the satirist who cannot escape the need to deny his age, like the idealist who suffers nothing but frustration for his dreams, so often takes refuge, like Orestes Brownson [2] and Hecker, after the hopes of Brook Farm, in the Roman Catho-

[1] Cf. F. O. Matthiessen, *American Renaissance* (London, 1942)—a remarkable work.

[2] Cf. Arthur Schlesinger, Jr., *Orestes A. Brownson: A Pilgrim's Progress* (New York, 1938).

lic Church. They yield their own insight to a traditional vision which will not admit the right to doubt. It is for them, like the Grand Inquisitor in *The Brothers Karamazov,* the means to an ultimate surrender of a faith that has lost all hope and can recognize freedom only in the prison-house that it enters.

"When morals cease to be a matter of tradition and orthodoxy," Mr. T. S. Eliot has written,[1] "that is, of the habits of the community, formulated, corrected and elevated by the continuous thought and direction of the Church—and when each man is to elaborate his own, then personality becomes a thing of alarming importance." It would be difficult to find a sentence which reveals more fully than this the final bankruptcy of our social order. For while it perceives that the moral quality of a system must be, as it were, a function of the community as natural to it as the phenomena of life and death, and while, too, it recognizes that the moral quality must change and grow, it assumes that its fate is to be entrusted to a Church and that the alternative is an individualism which rapidly assumes the character of a *Führer-prinzip*. Like his predecessor in fastidiousness, Henry James, he is appalled at the breakdown in values; but while James's judgment is a verdict upon that rich *bourgeoisie* whose devotion to property is their outstanding characteristic, the one in terms of which all the social relations of his novels are constructed, Mr. Eliot's judgment is a verdict upon the common people whose vulgarity so appals him that he is led by his distaste for them into hostility, as a critic, to poets like Milton who had played, even if only for a time, a progressive role in their age. Mr. Eliot does not ask himself what it is, alike in the ethical and intellectual record of the Church, that has made it incapable of retaining the guardianship of morals in our civilization. He does not examine its relation to the evolution of a tradition which has made personality "alarming in its importance." He merely looks backwards for the revival of a leadership which had risen and established its orthodoxy under cir-

[1] Cf. "Tradition and the Individual Talent" in T. S. Eliot, *Selected Essays* (1941), with *The Idea of a Christian Society* (1940).

cumstances completely different from those Mr. Eliot should himself have been observing. Henry James may not have understood that the morals of a society in which a small class of wealthy people are parasitic upon the labour of the masses are predestined to corruption; but, at least, he recognized the corruption when he encountered it. Mr. Eliot saw that same corruption; yet it did not occur to him that it could extend, as it had in fact for nearly two thousand years extended, to the very Church which he proposed to make the safeguard against its invasion of society. He did not understand that a Church which does not insist upon the inclusion of the masses within the culture of a civilization is bound to fail, in the long run, to perform that task of moral elevation he has assigned to it.

The truth is, of course, that the small, wealthy class had made the morals of our civilization no more than an argument for the defence of its own claims. As soon as the case against those claims was stated, with a force which, since the Industrial Revolution, has never ceased to gather momentum, it became increasingly obvious that they were ethically inadequate to the issues they sought to meet. They failed altogether to recognize the driving forces of the society in which they sought acceptance. It was really no use to ask that men should recognize how wretched they were, deformed by original sin, yet capable, as Mr. Eliot himself has said, of "apprehending perfection," if the working of the social and economic system in fact confines that apprehension—the idea of a Christian society—to a chosen few the very condition of whose existence as an *élite* is the inevitable exclusion of the overwhelming majority of men and women from the prospect even of being aware that such apprehension is possible. I think Mr. Eliot is wholly right in his view that the outcome of the moral decay he has seen so clearly and depicted with such incisive force is the glorification of power; and I think it is right to emphasize that when power, as such, has once been glorified, the emergence of the type like Hitler is only a matter of time and the occasion. But Hitler is, after all, no more than the final term in a series in which the feudal lord, the nobleman of the Renaissance, the aloof Whig aristocrat of eighteenth-century England, the Prussian general who built his conduct on the model of Frederick the Great, the ruthless millionaire of that America which had not yet finished the exploitation of the frontier, were also terms; and there was none of them with whom the Church, to which Mr. Eliot looks for liberation, was not willing eagerly to make its peace. If there is to be the chance of liberation, it is in other directions we must search.

For, at bottom, the Christian society of which Mr. Eliot writes so eloquently is not a means of liberating the masses, but a technique of escape for a few chosen souls who cannot bear the general spectacle of civilization in decay. It is a monastery, a retreat in the wilderness, which enables its inhabitants to turn their back upon the universe. That they are to do so in humble recognition of their miserable natures, I do not for one moment doubt Mr. Eliot believes; but I suggest that, beneath the announcement of humility, there is, as in Pascal, by whom it is evident that Mr. Eliot has been profoundly influenced, a limitless pride which recognizes with gratitude that the new Desert Fathers are not as other men are. And the plea, in any case, breaks down, partly because there is, in fact, no Church genuinely prepared to break with the world and thus surrender its hope of ultimately controlling the world, and, in part for the vital reason that, in the conditions of our time, that glorification of power which can result in the emergence of a Hitler means, inescapably, a totalitarian society in which the men who rule dare not allow the separate spiritual *élite* which Mr. Eliot recommends to us, since its very existence is an explicit criticism of their right to power. We are driven back, in short, not to the need to recover a tradition which our circumstances render an anachronism, but to the discovery of the principles which make a democratic society no longer a formality of use when rhetoric is in order, but a living reality which captures the heart and mind of the common man.

XVI

Conclusion

It is impossible, in the light of historical experience, to believe that there is the hope of salvation for humanity in a society where the exploited are to look to their exploiters for redemption. Their ways of life are too different; the common bond that links them together is too fragile not to break after a period of strain. Only in a social order where men know by the operation of its laws that the well-being of each is part of the well-being of the others, and not a subtraction from it, is there the effective right to look for enduring peace. There have been moments in history when, in an adventure which pushes the frontiers of experience beyond those limits which logic can control, some man, more deeply imaginative or more profoundly human than his contemporaries, has caught a glimpse of the road along which that adventure lies; just as there have been moments, too, when the depth of the insight that this glimpse has brought has communicated its own ecstasy to others, and built thereby the frontiers of our world nearer the road on which freedom can be found. I think it is probable that the disciples of Epicurus, when they sought to free the Roman world of the fears begotten by the pagan superstitions of their time, knew something of this ecstasy. One feels it again in the emotions of those first Christian communities which enabled them, in ardent fraternity, to await the Second Coming. And the creative power of that fraternity is surely shown by the constancy with which it is revived in the Church in each age when too passionate an absorption in the attainment of wealth seems to risk the danger of brutalizing mankind. Men like Peter Waldo and Saint Francis of Assisi were, whatever their faults of emphasis, seeking to make their generations understand that it is only in an intense caring for one's fellow-men that one obtains to genuine possession of oneself, and, thereby, to freedom.

But it is unlikely, as we survey the record of man's striving, that the secret of his salvation can be found either in some ascetic gospel, on the one hand, or in the building, on the other, of a special community within the framework of our common civilization. It is a constant experience that the ascetic inspiration does not endure, and that there is a level of material well-being which is indispensable, for most of us, to intellectual thought; all special communities, moreover, if they are in and part of the world become tainted by a quest for power destructive of their character, while, if they separate themselves from its normal life, tend to lack, when the first flush of enthusiasm has departed, the quality of inspiration from which they were born. Brook Farm and Icaria are, in the end, like Cîteaux and Cluny, a proof that those who separate themselves from their fellows have rarely enough enduring wisdom to make their example more than a faint gleam in the sky which few will see, and fewer still remember.

Lenin was surely right when the end he sought for was to build his heaven upon earth and to write the precepts of its faith into the inner fabric of a universal humanity. He was surely right, too, when he recognized that the prelude to peace is a war, and that it is futile to suppose that the tradition of countless generations can be changed, as it were, overnight. And he was not less right in his insistence that if the claims of a just and rational society are to prevail, those who believe in its claims must give it the strength and power out of which victory comes. The postulates upon which he built his dream were not new in the history of the race; what was new was that, for the first time, the man and the occasion and the conditions were all adjusted to one another in a harmony which neither the misery of violence nor the agony of civil war has been able to conceal. Despite all its cost in blood and toil and suffering, the dream has brought unbreakable hope to one-sixth of the surface of the world. It is not, of course, as yet, the fulfilment of the dream. But no one who compares the old Russian civilization, stagnant, pessimistic, convinced of its own futility, with the new, so energetic, so ardent, so confident in its aspirations, can easily deny that there is in the inner ethos of the Russian Revolution the clue to the secret which each race of men has ever pursued and from which it derives the dynamic of a revitalized freedom.

This is the stark issue that we confront. It could hardly be other than it is for men and women who stand, in terms of time, in the twilight of a culture which slowly moves towards the dawn of the age of science; it is important for us to remember that we cannot predict as yet the kind of day the sun will bring when it rises. All that we can do is to take honest account of our position, to insist that this new principle, whose march to power we are witnessing, is indeed a faith, which, if it creates temptations and difficulties such as have always accompanied the rise of a new faith, has yet been able to breed in the men and women who embrace it hope and exhilaration not less intense, and far more widespread, than any of its predecessors, that it has enabled them, in a real sense, to be born anew; and they draw from that re-creation the hope that they stand upon the threshold of an epoch of emancipation.

This is the stark issue we confront, above all the youth of our generation. It is not the issue of whether they have the courage to fight on to victory; already they have shown on a hundred battlefields how amply they possess that courage. It is the deeper problem of the use to which the victory is to be put, and whether they have the imagination to see that the future belongs to socialism. Like Heine, they may confess that they see socialism in control of the future only "with the utmost anxiety and uneasiness." Like him, too, they may "think only with fear and horror of the time when these dark iconoclasts will have gained power," and see in the victory of the proletariat the loss "of the old romantic world." Yet, like Heine, they must combine their fear with the admission of the "two voices that are raised in my breast in its favour, two voices which will not be silenced and are perhaps after all only devilish incitements, but however that may be, they dominate me and no power nor imagination can hold them in check. For the first of these voices is that of Logic. . . . I am ensnared by a terrible syllogism, and, if I cannot controvert the premise 'that all men have the right to eat,' I am forced to surrender to all its consequences. . . . I cry aloud: 'It has been judged and condemned for long, the old social order, let it meet its due. Let it be destroyed, the old world, where cynicism flourished, and man was exploited by man. Let them be utterly destroyed, those whited sepulchres, where lies and injustice dwelt.' . . . The second of these two tyrant voices . . . is that of hatred, of the hatred which I have for the party whose most terrible antagonist is Communism, the party which for this reason is our common foe. I mean the party of the professed representatives of nationalism . . . those sham patriots whose love for the Fatherland is only a foolish prejudice against foreigners and neighbouring peoples. . . . I find comfort in the conviction that Communism, which will find them its first enemies in the way, will give them the *coup de grâce*."

We must learn to find that comfort, too; for it is only as the victory is devoted to these ends that it is either real or lasting. We must not deceive ourselves; our task only begins on the day when our enemies lay down their arms, and we may fear that the "dark iconoclasts" of the new order make us spend what seems like an effort as hard as war itself in the building of the socialist society. But if we learn to find that comfort, we can learn, as Heine's imagination enabled him nearly a century ago, amid all the fears and the anxieties of the struggle, to find the promise of a new dawn. "Yes," he wrote,[1] "it will be a splendid day when the sun of liberty makes the earth warmer and happier than all the stars of the aristocracy put together; a new generation will spring up, begotten in freedom and love, not in constraint and the control of publicans and priests. Born in freedom, men will come into the world with thoughts and feelings so free that we who are born slaves have no idea of them.

[1] This, and the preceding quotations are from the preface, dated March 30, 1855, to Heine's *Lutetia*. I have made some small omissions.

They will little know how terrible was the night, in the darkness of which we had to live, and how cruelly we were forced to fight against hideous ghosts, and shrieking owls, and sanctimonious sinners. Oh! the poor struggling wretches that we are, compelled to waste our lifetime in such a fight, so that we are weary and pale when the day of victory dawns. The glow of the sunrise will no longer colour our cheeks, and our hearts will never more be kindled into warmth; we pass and die away like the waning moon. All too short is the way of man's pilgrimage, and at the end of it lies the inexorable grave."

Our generation, certainly, dare not hope to enter the promised land; it must be enough for us if we labour to set the feet of our children on the road at whose end it lies. For only by an effort to make possible everywhere the coming of that day of freedom can we deem ourselves entitled, a second time within a single generation, to call the youth of the whole world to the risk of death. Only as our achievement for those who come after us seeks some genuine proportion to the sacrifice we exact from them, shall we receive acquittal at the bar of history.